"In my latest book, *Bullet‌[proof]*

Business and Your Family, ... troduce the term "Value Catalyst" to describe structures and strategies that have an exponential impact on organizations. A Value Catalyst is a process or person that creates much more energy, time, and money than it takes in. Implementing Value Catalysts can truly change the direction and the quality of your life and help you build a true Bulletproof Business.

Scott Danner knows the levers needed to find your Value Catalysts as a financial advisor. He has the track record to prove it. He has worked with many advisors to help them realize their potential and ultimately exit their practices. You don't want to miss the exponential impact Scott can have on you and your organization. This is likely the most relevant book you will ever read related to your lasting success in your profession as a financial advisor. If you want to make a huge difference in your business, your family, and your profession, I highly recommend you read this book.

—Randy M. Long, JD, CFP®, CExP™

Author of *The BraveHeart Exit: 7 Steps to Your Family Business Legacy* and *Bulletproof Your Exit: How to Prepare Your Business and Your Family for a Successful Business Exit.*

Founder of Long Business Advisors, LLC and President of Long Family Office, Inc.

FREEDOM STREET

freedom
STREET

HOW I LEARNED TO CREATE A RICH LIFE,
LIVE MY LEGACY, AND OWN THE
FUTURE AS A FINANCIAL ADVISOR

SCOTT DANNER

LIONCREST
PUBLISHING

Freedom Street: How I Learned to Create a Rich Life, Live My Legacy, and Own the Future as a Financial Advisor

Hardcover ISBN: 978-1-5445-2216-6
Paperback ISBN: 978-1-5445-2215-9
eBook ISBN: 978-1-5445-2214-2
Audiobook ISBN: 978-1-5445-2217-3

To Adrienne and our boys.
I am so grateful for the love and support.
To my parents for helping me to become the man
I am still becoming.
And to Aunt Paulette for getting me into the industry.

Contents

Foreword

by Steve Moeller, Author of
Effort-Less Marketing for Financial Advisors and
Endorphinomics: The Science of Human Flourishing

Like most people, I instantly liked Scott Danner when we first met. He had read my book, *Effort-Less Marketing for Financial Advisors*, and called to learn about my management consulting services. We immediately connected and Scott soon hired me to help reinvent his business.

I was impressed by three things about Scott: 1) his passion for helping others; 2) he understood and valued my client-centered approach to business building; and 3) he had built a successful investment business the "hard way" and was eager to try a new and more rewarding approach.

Scott wanted to add more value for his clients and to make a bigger impact in his community. He also wanted more quality time with his family. Most importantly, he understood that businesses only grow when their leaders grow.

We worked on Scott's business for several years. He reevaluated every aspect of his operation. He learned to see the world from his clients' perspective, as opposed to his firm's perspective. He discovered that many of his clients yearned for permission to pursue deeply held dreams and aspirations. Scott helped them go confidently and prudently in the direction of their dreams. His insights guided him as he upgraded his services, systemized his business processes, and transformed his marketing strategies.

An eager student, Scott was the only financial advisor in my 25 years of consulting who studied all 50 of my learning modules! He applied the ideas that made sense to him. He even embraced my research on the power of positive emotions and my strategies for enhancing life satisfaction. Always a coach, as Scott was learning to build a better business, he was mentoring and coaching other advisors in his firm.

Scott is one of my most successful clients because he integrated many of my client-centered strategies into his business processes. And he personalized them to capitalize on his unique passions and strengths. The result of all of Scott's work over about four years was a quantum leap in the value of his business and the quality of his life. He basically delegated everything but his most enjoyable activities and essential responsibilities.

Like all of my clients, Scott eventually graduated from my *Visionary Advisory* program. But he continued to learn, grow, hire other consultants, and focus on helping even more people. In this book, Scott shares how he created the perfect business—for his unique personality and passions. He offers inspiration and a path forward for advisors who want a better business, a better life— and a better future.

This is an inspiring, true story of one successful financial advisor's journey from grinding it out to enjoying a deeply rewarding career and a fulfilling life.

Prepare to be engaged, entertained, and maybe even enlightened as you read Scott's inspiring story of business mastery and personal fulfillment.

—Steve Moeller, Auburn, CA, 2021

Introduction

If you believe in reincarnation, pray that you come back as the first-born grandson in an Italian Catholic family full of women. You are Simba—the chosen one. And you're spoiled rotten. Not with toys, but with the perfect amount of *attention*.

That was me. Thinking back, I can almost imagine my mother and grandmother holding me up like the treasured cub in *The Lion King*. Surrounded by all my mom's sisters; my uncle, John; and a Sicilian grandmother who thought the world revolved around me, I could do no wrong, and if I did and Dad tried to discipline me, the women came to my rescue. It would take me many years to figure out that Dad knew what he was doing all along and I probably didn't deserve rescuing!

I had no idea how lucky I was to be so loved, so supported, and to have so many people looking out for me. I was too young to realize it, but thanks to all that love, my confidence and self-esteem were through the roof. I felt as if I could accomplish anything. I was also developing a strong sense of understanding and respect for other people, especially women. Listening to them talk about what was important to them—conversations young men are typically not privy to—set me up with a unique insight into what people talk about with those they trust.

The talents, gifts, and skills I was developing made me very good at what I did early in my career as a financial advisor and now as CEO of Freedom Street Partners. My financial practice not only helps clients reach their financial goals; we also specialize in helping advisors through the many stages of their careers. This includes pairing younger advisors who are looking for growth and mentorship with more experienced professionals, as well as guiding seasoned advisors through the latter stages of their careers and preparing them for the next stage, whatever that may be.

Back then, I wasn't aware my my early experiences gave me an advantage that would pay off immensely later in life. They made me a better husband and father, and they contributed to my success. You may have had similar experiences or very different ones that have made *you* very good at what you do. After all, if you've been an advisor for any length of time, you must be doing something right. You have a talent for connecting, a gift for communicating, and you're skilled at building relationships. Something inside you makes you very good at truly helping people—not just financially, but personally.

But while your clients appreciate and respect you— maybe even love you—for all that you do for them, *you are probably not applying that same level of care and attention to yourself.* I know I wasn't. Not at first. I started my career the way most financial advisors begin theirs—gung-ho to succeed. I leveraged my gifts and made tremendous financial strides early on, but something was missing. I wanted more of *something* from my work—not just money, but something more for myself. And maybe something for others, too.

No matter what numbers I made, no matter what success ratios I hit, there was an emptiness inside me that wasn't being filled. I was unsatisfied with the path I was on, but gradually, I figured out how to turn my self-confidence and compassion for others into a life that served a higher purpose, and ultimately brought me more love, happiness, and comfort than I could have ever imagined. It's the same kind of comfort I enjoyed as a kid, surrounded by my wonderful family.

I'm an advisor who's learned how to create a rich life, live my legacy, and own my future. That's not to say I've got it all figured out. I don't (far from it!). But I know what's working for me, and I've seen firsthand how it's helped other advisors. And I'm *still* learning every day.

In this book, I'm going to tell you how I did it and how you can do it too. Like me, you'll see how to use your talents, gifts, and skills to make your work more satisfying. I believe that each of us has our own unique value proposition that we can leverage every day to be the best at what we do.

What makes you different? How do you stand out? I bet that if we were having this conversation face-to-face and I asked you these questions, you would immediately light up! You'd want to share your answers with me. Unfortunately, people don't go around asking each other the important questions. Even worse, we don't ask ourselves. If, however, you start thinking about yourself and all the value you bring to others in new and powerful ways, you'll find more fulfillment in your life and work. You'll move forward and escape the comfortable box of success that you've been operating in for years, maybe decades. You'll discover that you're capable of a whole lot more.

You may have to dig deep or look into your past to figure out your special sauce. Self-awareness is a beautiful thing. Understanding where your strengths lie (and where you might be lacking—what I call a blind spot) isn't limiting— it's liberating. Identifying and acknowledging what you're really good at, and where you need a little help, frees you to move forward at full throttle today and into your next stage.

PLANNING *YOUR* FUTURE

I love helping people plan for the future. It's my favorite part of the job: helping clients do what needs to be done right now so they don't have to worry about what comes next. I truly believe that most financial advisors feel the same way. So it came as a shock to me when I discovered that so many of my colleagues have no plans for their *own* futures. On top of that, they are so wrapped up in their work and in getting ahead, that the most important things in their lives are set aside. It's as if we think we'll have time for all those things later, instead of building our lives and careers around them now.

Successful advisors make a great living, especially in a good economy. We do *so* well financially that sometimes we forget about everything else—like family, and friendships, and how we could be making an incredible impact on the lives of people in our communities and creating a living, lasting legacy. Successful advisors can tend to have a distorted vision about what happens after their own lifetime of work. They struggle with real clarity or direction for what comes next. Where do we go from here when we want to retire? Do we sell our business? Merge with another firm? Is one of our kids going to take it over? How is *that* even going to work?

When everything's going well, it's easy to put those decisions aside. But sooner or later we have to deal with them. And I'll tell you, after forcing myself to consider these decisions and helping many advisors work through their own next stage, I've learned that the sooner we start to deal with them, the better. Like right now. Today. Because later is going to be here a lot sooner than you think, and the longer you wait to prepare for tomorrow, the more limited your options will become.

When circumstances force you to make a decision, it's harder to decide. You feel rushed. You don't have the luxury of time to weigh all your options, and those options may be far fewer than they were just a couple of years ago. This is why you need to take stock now of where you are and how that affects where you could be in the future. Then you can make decisions on your own timeline, with more options and more time to consider and compare them, leading to better results.

The key is to act now—today. Waiting could put you in a position that's less than ideal, where that dream you had simmering in the back of your mind of a rich life, a lasting legacy, and a purposeful, fulfilling next stage slips through your fingers, all because you waited just a little too long.

> The Dalai Lama, when asked what surprised him most about humanity, answered "Man! Because he sacrifices his health in order to make money. Then he sacrifices money to recuperate his health. And then he is so anxious about the future that he does not enjoy the present; the result being that he does not live in the present or the future; he lives as if he is never going to die, and then dies having never really lived."

WHAT'S NEXT

The good news is that most advisors still have time to take control of their next stage. In this book, I'll give you the guidance to own your future while creating a richer life for yourself now. It's never too late to do something about your impact in the world today, or the future you have yet to enjoy.

I'll show you how to shift your focus from dollars to sense and go from Wall Street to Freedom Street. Ultimately, that's what this is all about: *discovering what freedom means to you and then making it happen in your life.*

I'll also tell you some stories from my own life. It's important to remember, as I'm looking back on my past and how it helped me understand how I became the man, husband, father, business owner, financial advisor, and author I am today, that I'm still growing. This is still a journey for me, and I have more to learn, but I can share what I've learned to this point and where I am on that journey today. Some of these experiences are business-related, while others are quite personal. Reflecting on these events, my responses to them, and the outcomes provides me with insights into why I care about the things I care about and why I'm so driven to help others. My hope is that, by providing these examples, I'll inspire you to revisit your own experiences and gain a better understanding of why you are driven to do what you do in this business—basically, why being the best advisor you can be to those who depend on you is so important.

Although I wrote this book for financial advisors, the concepts apply to anyone in a professional career who's looking ahead at their next chapter. Any business owner can benefit from these lessons, whether they're a doctor, a lawyer, or an entrepreneur—this book is for people who are very good at what they do and typically have long, rewarding careers. They aren't eager to give up their professional lives, but they want to know what's next for them in life.

Regardless of your profession, you have something more to offer the world now and in your next stage. You may have to do some soul-searching to figure out what that is, just as I did. I had to go way back to figure out how I had become this person who cared so much about other people and their outcomes—cared enough to become a leading advisor who loves my job, loves the people I serve, yet strives to do even more with what I have to offer.

In Part 1, "Creating a Rich Life," we'll talk about the challenges advisors face that stand in the way of having a truly happy and fulfilled life. I'll show you how to rediscover what matters most, and how to find a perfect balance between what you want to do and what you have to do to be happy and successful, while setting yourself up for what comes next.

In Part 2, "Living Your Legacy," you'll discover how to start making your legacy today, instead of waiting until the end of your career. We'll talk about what you have to offer the world that no one else has, and how you can start making a difference for people and the causes you care about. We'll discuss what you can be doing differently to create a legacy that makes the world a better place today and will have a lasting impact for generations to come.

In Part 3, "Owning Your Future," we'll get into the details of your next stage. We'll examine all the exit strategy choices and explore what you should be doing now to prepare for the option that's right for you.

Come along with me and I'll tell you how I did this for myself while helping other advisors do the same. Part of my plan included launching a wine festival that's generated millions of dollars for local charities right here in my community.

Are you smiling? Keep smiling, because you can do that, too, or something like it. Let's talk about how you're going to get there. But first, let's talk about where you are right now and how you can make it so much better.

PART I

Creating a Rich Life

The meaning of life is to find your gift.
The purpose of life is to give it away.
—Pablo Picasso

While I was putting one of my kids to bed the other night, he asked me, "Dad, would you be rich if you didn't have us?"

I burst out laughing—not at my son, but at the absurdity of the question. I cannot even *imagine* my life without my family in it. But this was the perfect opportunity to talk to him about what having a "rich life" means to me.

"Well," I said, "*rich* is a really interesting word. Would I be *financially* rich without you guys? Yeah, I'd have a lot more money than I do right now, but my life would be pretty empty. Without something or someone to care about, where I can put my money, I couldn't be rich. So no matter how much I spend supporting you and your brother, I'm way richer *with* you than *without* you."

This sums up what it means to me to have a rich life. Sure, having money is great. Having something or someone to care about is better. Having the means to invest in the causes I believe in and people I love is the best. As financial advisors, we often overlook the connection between what's important to us and how we can use our position and assets to make those things better and, in effect, make our own lives that much richer.

That's what Part 1, "Creating a Rich Life," is all about. In the following three chapters, we'll discuss the challenges you and other advisors face in creating a rich, fulfilled life; the steps you can take to bring more of what you love into your life; and how you can strike that perfect balance between what you want and need to do to create the rich life you deserve.

CHAPTER 1

On the Road to Riches

Money can buy you comfort, but it can't buy you peace.
Money can buy you pleasure, but it can't buy you happiness.
Money can buy you food, but it can't buy you contentment.
Money can buy you delight, but it can't buy you love.
—Matshona Dhliwayo

Can't buy me love.
—John Lennon and Paul McCartney

The first year I broke $100,000, I got a "Century Award" at the firm where I worked. It was a huge milestone for me, and the message was abundantly clear: Make money, and you are a success. Make more money, and you are a bigger success.

In our industry, everything is defined by money: how much you bring in, how much you make, and how much you make for your clients. We are defined by our financial markers. This is what we celebrate as advisors. It's what I celebrated, and still do to an extent. While I can't dismiss the benefits of financial success, this culture can lead advisors to believe that making money is the only value we have in life.

Of course, I've known plenty of advisors who have never viewed money as their "God." I certainly never did. There is a difference between doing what's right and celebrating your success, and simply celebrating the money and all the material benefits that come with it. Yet, looking back on how I started, I had plenty of shallow thoughts about what mattered in life. I wanted the big home with the pool. I wanted the fancy car and the lavish vacations. There is nothing wrong with wanting any of those things as long as you realize there are more important things to go after, and that sometimes those flashy things that grab your attention come at a cost, and not just financially. You pay for all those high-priced items—life's little accoutrements—with time and energy, which are limited resources that you could be devoting to life's real riches: friends, family, relationships, and serving a higher purpose.

Life, if well lived, is long enough.
—Lucius Annaeus Seneca

Focusing on those things that don't really matter and convincing yourself that they are proof of your value can cost you your freedom, too. I'm not talking about being locked away because you have nice things, but you have to pay for them, and that often means putting in a lot of hours at your desk when you could be doing something else. I had seen advisors in this situation, and I did not want to join their ranks.

On the other end of the spectrum, I knew advisors who had gotten to a certain place in their careers and slowed down so much, I was surprised they stayed in business. That may have been why I drove myself so hard for so long— the fear of being like them, and letting myself, my team, my clients, and my family down. Because it didn't go well for those advisors.

More often, advisors are somewhere in the middle of that spectrum. They love their families and want to do well for them personally and financially. But maybe they've leaned a bit too much into work, or too far away from it. They just need some guidance to help them get on the right track.

HARDWORKING HANK

Hank was a financial advisor who worked all the time— evening, weekends, holidays...you get the picture. The business had taken over his life. When I met "Hardworking Hank" at a national conference, he was totally defeated. At the time, the government was considering the Department of Labor (DOL) fiduciary rule, which had the potential to have a massive impact on how some advisors do business. Investment policy statements; defined goals, objectives, and boundaries for investing; a documented financial plan; and even risk tolerance would need to be documented a certain way. Even seasoned professionals who had great practices and had always put the client first didn't necessarily have the proper systems and processes in place that regulators would require moving forward. Hank was afraid the new DOL rule would put him out of business. He didn't have the practices and processes in place that would have made his work more repeatable, efficient, and effective, and he was always behind the curve as a result.

He was making good money, but his business was very transaction driven. The practice had *so much* more potential for growth! Hank was also a single, divorced dad with two children. He wanted to be present with the people he cared about, but at the end of the day, work left him depleted.

Where you spend all your time is where you put all your love, and that takes away all the love you could be giving to something or someone else. Putting all your love into something that doesn't love you back—like a job—is a sure way to end up alone. Sure, the job was liking Hank a lot with a paycheck, but all the money in the world won't give a person what they really need, which is to be heard, understood, valued, and loved.

Don't get me wrong. I love *making* money and enjoy having financial freedom. But if at my memorial, anyone starts the eulogy with "Scott loved money," I swear I will rise up and smite them down. I love life, and I love my wife and my sons, and I kind of love wine. I love many people and things, and most of them love me back. That was the difference between me and Hank: he wasn't directing his love in the right direction. The divorce didn't even wake him up, but the thought of losing the one thing he had sunk all his love into—his business—had him terrified.

I could tell that Hank needed someone to talk to. "After being an advisor for twenty-five years, what's your quality of life like?" I asked.

Hank sunk in his chair and said, "Honestly, I haven't had a vacation in years. I don't take time off or spend enough quality time with my kids. I'm extremely worried about the regulatory environment that we're going into and that my practice is not positioned. I don't have a good mentor relationship. The connectivity I had early in my career was with a guy who has been in the business more than forty years, and at this point, his way of working is outdated and he's in just as bad a shape as I am." Hank told me about his office. "I've got files all over the place and an assistant who answers the phone while I do most of the heavy lifting."

I don't try to tell people what to do with their businesses unless they ask, and Hank was on life support. He was ready to throw in the towel on being an advisor, and at fifty years old, he didn't know where that would leave him. "Can you help me?" he asked.

"I'm concerned about the amount of work that needs to be done," I told him, "but I know you always put your clients first, and that's why I want to work with you. That's how I work too." The systems and processes I would introduce Hank to would be uncomfortable at first, and I had to know that he trusted me enough to change how he did business. "If you want my help," I said, "you have to promise me that we'll do it the right way."

Hank nodded, and that's how our business relationship and our friendship began.

LAID-BACK LONNIE

Lonnie was another kind of financial advisor. He worked steadily and got to a point where he had an annual income in the low six-figure range without having to do much. He'd come in late, leave early, and had a pretty good life/work balance. "Laid-Back Lonnie" had a big house and a nice car, and his suits were tailored. He took his family on lavish vacations. But Lonnie was like a lot of other advisors I've known who get to this point: he wasn't really getting anywhere. He had eased off the throttle so much, he was basically treading water. Guys like this come into work around 10 a.m., take lunch, then work for another couple of hours *but they don't really do much in the four hours they're at work.*

*A man who dares to waste one hour of time
has not discovered the value of life.*
—Chares Darwin

Some people can put in a four-hour workday and bust out a ton of work. Others, like Lonnie, get so comfortable that they squander those few hours. These are the people who call me midmorning to see if I watched the Ohio State game the night before. *What? It's 10 a.m.,* I'm thinking, *and I'm in the middle of the most productive part of my day.* I used to think guys like Lonnie had it all figured out and that's why they could afford to goof off. But the truth is, these guys are having problems. They may appear rich in every sense of the word, but many feel the weight of their mortgage and car payments. They haven't figured out how they're going to pay for that high-end European vacation for their wife (or husband) this summer or Johnny's college tuition in the fall.

In this industry, just getting by and paying the bills isn't making it. Advising clients on financial matters one way while living and working by a different set of rules isn't authentic. Imagine how that feels to an advisor as he lays his head on the pillow at night. Deep inside, he knows something's not quite right. Yet, advisors who live and work this way see themselves as great successes—and they keep riding that wave until it crashes.

When your time comes to die, be not like those whose hearts are filled with fear of death, so that when their time comes they weep and pray for a little more time to live their lives over again in a different way. Sing your death song, and die like a hero going home.
—Chief Tecumseh

LIFE/WORK BALANCE

Hank and Lonnie are two sides of the same coin, but their vision was equally clouded. Hank thought hard work and money would fulfill him, while Lonnie had convinced himself that once he "made it," he could relax, as if the mere image of success would sustain him. They were both wrong.

If Hank and Lonnie stayed on their paths, they would never create a rich life, live their legacies, and own their futures. They were on two different paths to the same place: nowhere. They had no idea what freedom meant, or what being rich meant. Because they hadn't figured that out—asked themselves those questions—they were both trapped somewhere else. In Hank's case, the trap was a job; in Lonnie's, it was a lifestyle that he couldn't sustain. But neither of them knew how to escape the traps they'd created for themselves.

Life/work balance seems to be an important topic for working people, yet no one actually talks about it, at least honestly. Financial advisors *especially* don't talk about it. The Hardworking Hanks in our business—who are motivated intrinsically and succeed by literally outworking everybody else—work themselves to financial success, but that's the only success they have. The Laid-Back Lonnies—who are motivated extrinsically by a need to constantly prove their material wealth to the world—keep their heads above water just enough to buy (or lease) the next new car, or boat, or home. To the outsider, these guys look like tremendous successes. Hank and Lonnie like to pretend they're successful, too, but when they're being honest with themselves—and I mean really coming clean with who they are and how they feel every day—they know they're trapped. With no real freedom, their realities are not living up to their dreams. Remember, though: *most advisors still have time to take control of their next stage. It's never too late to do something about the future you have yet to enjoy.* That's true for most advisors. Some stay Lonnies forever. As for Hank, well, we'll revisit his story a little later in this book.

GOOD FRIENDS, GOOD BOURBON, AND AN EPIPHANY

In my twenties, I had set a goal for myself to make over $100,000 a year by the time I was thirty—which, at the time, seemed like a huge accomplishment—and I had beat my goal by several years. Getting that Century Award meant *a lot*. So I set a new goal to have a net worth of $1 million by the time I was forty, and I beat that one too. Exceeding expectations was fundamental to me, and I couldn't allow myself to settle for anything less.

My life and career sure seemed to be going as planned. But something was off; I was beginning to see things differently. Those financial goals didn't become less important, but other goals that didn't have anything to do with money took on a greater significance.

The idea had been tickling my brain for months, but I'd never discussed it with anyone. (Advisors don't talk about things like that, right?) I headed into my fortieth birthday feeling like everything was going so well yet something was *off*. I didn't realize that what was bothering me would come into focus by the end of the day.

My wife had set up a trip to Bourbon Country, Kentucky, for me and nine of my best friends, my brother, and guys from my college days. We sipped bourbon and talked about all those things we had stopped talking about in our twenties because we were working so hard to get ahead, and in our thirties because we had so many obligations—work, family, homeownership, finances, and everything else that filled our days. On this day, we talked about *life*.

That was when it came to me: something I had known all along yet had let get away from me. I was reminded that my relationships were more valuable than anything else in my life, and that the best relationships I had were those that had matured, like a fine wine—or top-shelf bourbon—with age. If I wanted to foster those rich relationships, I had to put more time into them. Hyper-focused on the day-to-day life and work of a financial advisor, I wasn't making enough quality time for conversations with friends, or for any of the people I needed more of in my life. I have always prioritized relationships, but years of shifting time away from them and toward career goals had caused my dearest friendships to suffer. There was so much more value to the human connections I had made with people—with my wife, my kids, my friends, colleagues, and clients—than could ever be reflected in my bank account.

Maybe it was the bourbon. Maybe it was being around old friends, remembering what it was like to talk about something other than the day-to-day. In the past, those things had been important to me, and I had let them slip away. Starting a business had consumed all my time, and even though I was growing the practice and helping a lot of advisors and clients, I had sacrificed a part of me that I needed to protect. It was as if the pilot light had gone out of that best part of me and had to be relit.

We advisors focus on production awards, rankings, and the money that's coming in, and often judge one another not by our character, but by how well we are doing—or rather, how much we think the other one makes. "Gosh, you're killing it, Scott. You're making a ton!"

Of course, they have no idea how much money I make, or how much I put back into the business, or what I spend to grow it. They don't know how much I give away, either. But still, this is how we classify one another. I don't fault people who do this. It's part of our culture, and I'm just as guilty as the next guy of having these thoughts. However, I'd like to believe I've grown over the years. I'm constantly working to change my way of thinking, because I and every other advisor have much more to offer the world than a pile of money.

PERPETUATING THE MONEY MYTH

I was never a money-hungry asshole. As driven and super-focused as I was, I was also grounded and never forgot what it was like for the "new guys/gals." I empathized with them and what they were going through, and we had nicknames for each other that helped us describe what the business was like at each stage. These monikers typically correlated with how long an advisor had been in the business and their level of success. Mostly, it was about the level of personal and financial freedom we had achieved.

"Monday" and "Tuesday" advisors were grinding away and barely getting anywhere. They always seemed to be behind everyone else and never able to catch up; that's how it is when you're first starting out. They weren't making six figures yet (and by the way, if you're not making at least that much in this business, you're a Monday/Tuesday advisor), and they had a ways to go, if they stuck it out.

"Wednesday" or "Hump Day" advisors had good months and bad, but they sometimes scraped their way to six figures. Some of these advisors weren't consistent in their efforts and had uneven results that rose and fell on the highs and lows of a fluctuating market. New business would come in, and they'd work like crazy, but when business slowed, they'd get frustrated and sometimes give up. Other Hump Day advisors worked hard all the time, but they just hadn't been at it long enough to make it to "Thursday," while still others had occasional "Fridays."

"Thursday" and "Friday" advisors set their own schedules. They had worked their way to a very high income and were even comfortable enough to golf a couple times a week with clients. These advisors had settled into a routine that was easy enough and made them plenty of money, so they weren't thinking past Friday. Sure, many of them had terrific lives: beautiful families, gorgeous homes, lots of vacations, and everything else that most people see as markers of a successful life; but many were leaving a lot of value on the table. They had so much more to give to the world and receive in return. Maybe some of them were thinking about it. Back then, I was *always* thinking about it; I just didn't know the path forward—the one that would eventually lead me to financial freedom.

Wherever you are on your financial journey, as long as you're moving forward, you likely have a good career going in this business. But I want you to think about something else, beyond the financial success. I've known people in "every day of the week" and at every stage in their career, and what I've discovered is this: when you define your value, your *worth*, to yourself and others solely in financial terms, it gets very difficult to imagine what else you have to offer the world. And that, my friend, is not a good place to be.

Never confuse net worth for self-worth.
—Keith J. Cunningham, author of *The Road Less Stupid*

Yet that's where so many of us begin, and often continue, for our entire careers. Some of us are driven to generate as much money as possible to prove our worth, while others define our value simply through our hard work. It's not enough to *have* enough—we actually feel worthless whenever we take a break. "I should be doing more" is the mantra—code for working more and/or making more money. Every truly entrepreneurial person I've met shares that burning desire; it's quite possibly what drives us to start our own business or become an advisor in the first place.

Early in my career, I actually believed this too. At my first firm, I knocked on doors to find new clients, with the goal of speaking to twenty-five people a day. Even though I loved talking to people, the door-to-door stuff could have been awful. I made a game of it by telling myself that if I knocked on just one more door, I'd find that wonderful new client. I focused on the good people and dismissed the bad as just another "necessary no" that I had to rack up to get enough yeses. I pushed myself to do it: *keep walking, keep knocking, keep talking*. That constant push gets under your skin, and you keep going, thinking that one magic door will open—or enough doors will open—and you'll be on the road to success. It's hard to stop.

THE ILLUSION OF WEALTH

Financial advisors are very conscious of how we present ourselves to others. We want to inspire confidence, which means dressing well. On the other hand, we don't want to appear as if we spend money foolishly.

One day I drove my 2004 Dodge Ram truck to meet a client. A bank was buying out a mortgage company, and some of their wealthier clients were accepting buyouts. A client had referred me to the event, and I was invited to present to a group of about a dozen people affected.

I had bought the truck used, and it was in fair shape, just not the kind of vehicle you'd expect to see a guy driving to a million-dollar deal. After some good conversations with potential customers, one of them continued our discussion out to the parking lot. When we got to my beat-up truck, I saw the look on his face and imagined his thoughts, *I'm trusting my money to a guy who can't even afford a bed liner for his truck?*

I was painfully aware of how it looked, but I've heard about worse situations. Like the advisor who buys the flashy car and drives out to the country to meet with a rancher who's worked every day of his life, and led a very humble, frugal existence. The rancher sees this BMW coming up the driveway and thinks, *This guy's making too much money, blowing it on a car like this, and I'm going to trust him with my money?*

This is the conundrum, and what a lot of people would call a first-world problem. But the bottom line is, we advisors put a lot of pressure on ourselves and each other to exude an image of wealth, and some of our clients expect that too. But unless that's the real you, the authentic you, that image doesn't cut it. If you're showing off your silver cufflinks and designer suit around the office, that's great. But think about who you're wearing them for—you might impress your colleagues and certain clients, but you could be alienating others. Being yourself—whether that's Dodge truck guy or BMW gal—is the best way to go.

Standing outside the bank that day, my worries about my old truck and prospective client, as it turned out, were unwarranted. "Ah, you're a Dodge man," he said. "They really hold their value, don't they?"

Then he added, "So what's your schedule like next week?"

THE BALANCING ACT NO ONE TALKS ABOUT

Everyone who works goes through a balancing act. We balance work and life, work and family, and all the individual demands of work, life, and family. Nothing's worse than leaving the office on time feeling like you didn't accomplish anything, or staying late knowing you're missing out on precious family time. But that's what happens when we don't make the conscious effort to learn what matters to us, or the conscious decision to make it a priority.

We all talk about life/work balance, but no one talks about the discipline required to create and maintain it. That lack of discipline is a weakness that no one wants to own up to. I'll talk more about discipline in the coming chapters. For now, consider how being more disciplined in how you spend your time creates more freedom in your life and more opportunities for great achievement. And realize that most people struggle with actually *being* disciplined. We all see the value in it and want to do it, but following through—that's the real challenge. (Think about the discipline required to lose weight!)

Early in your career, when you're in an environment surrounded by a lot of people in the business, accountability partners are everywhere. You can't goof off—people are watching. They're looking at you and your numbers. When you move away from that environment—whether you're an independent advisor or you have your own practice— discipline is even *more* imperative. With no one looking over your shoulder, listening over the cubicle, or sharing stories at the coffee machine, it's on *you* to hold *yourself* accountable. And the more you have on your plate, the more critical it becomes to first, identify what's important and second, find the discipline to focus on it.

Even advisors who look like they have all the discipline in the world and have mastered that elusive life/work balance haven't necessarily got it all figured out. The further you are in your career, the more likely you are to believe that it's just you who's struggling, but that's not the case. Out of that environment and on your own, you just aren't seeing it anymore.

START TO FIND YOUR BALANCE

I admit, I've painted a pretty bleak picture for advisors. You're probably thinking that finding the discipline to create more balance in your life isn't possible, so why bother? Because living a rich life is within every advisor's grasp. And the solution isn't even that complicated. In fact, in rebalancing my own life and working with other advisors to find discipline and balance in their lives, I've discovered that many of us share the same barriers that prevent us from getting there.

So much of our work is unpredictable. We deal with people and the many changes in their lives that affect their finances, and despite our best forecasts and plans, we don't always know what will change from one day to the next. Clients are the true variable—the wild card. We never know what may come up, but we can prepare. You may have a client who suddenly passes away, and you spend hours with the spouse working through all the details of their finances while also being emotionally supportive and sensitive to their situation. That's mentally and physically draining, and you're not always prepared for it. You can't create predictability in your clients' lives, but you can create it on the backend so you have something to rely on that helps balance it out. Systems around time, processes, scalability, and compliance help you control what you can control, and offset the inherent inconsistencies of your work. So let's talk more about the most common obstacles holding us back at work, and begin to look at some solutions. Acknowledging the problems, after all, is the first step to solving them.

Time

At the start of my career, I was more of a fireman than an advisor. I allowed my clients to dictate my schedule, and this is a common approach for a lot of new advisors. In the beginning, you're so eager to bring in new business that you say yes to everything, and instead of running a business, your business is running you. Once I realized what I was doing to myself, I began setting boundaries that allowed me to take back control of my time. This isn't about saying no—it's about identifying the value of your time and deciding how to invest it to best serve the people you want to serve.

This is also about recognizing your strengths and playing to them. I want you to listen closely here because this is very important: everybody has strengths, and yours are what have made you successful so far. Think about what you're best at as a financial advisor—what makes you light up. Do you love talking to clients about how they took their grandkids to see their favorite NFL team, and how you can help them with a plan that allows them more time and money to enjoy more of that in their life? Or do you light up when you have time alone to analyze the data, slice and dice the numbers, and do some intense problem-solving? Your strengths are the key components to building a rich life, and where you should be focusing most of your time at work.

If you're spending all your time at the computer, that leaves no time for clients, which is fine if computer work lights you up, and there's someone else in the office who loves talking to people. Reassess your strengths, and then reorder your priorities. Part of having a rich life is developing a life/work balance, but it's also enjoying what you do when you are at work. Otherwise, work becomes a chore.

Through the years of failing forward and revealing what I love to do, I've built my role around those activities I enjoy most: leadership, mentoring, coaching, recruiting, and being the visionary. I love the one-on-one conversations with clients and other advisors, and that's where I want to spend my time. As the CEO of a company, I know where my blind spots are, too, and I have people to fill them. We're all much happier that way, and the business—and our clients— are better off for it.

Processes

Processes aren't typically developed early enough in a new business, and a lot of time is wasted because of the delay. If you do something every day or every week or every month—or with any degree of regularity—the task will go faster and be easier with a process or standard operating procedure (SOP) stating when you do it, why you do it, and how you do it. Just having a goal for every call or email will take you a lot further than winging it.

Have you thought about putting together a process for calling your clients, including how often you call them and the desired outcome? Have an agenda and a schedule before you hit the dial button. You can do this with your favorite CRM system. Having a logical process to follow makes the job more efficient and makes you more productive.

Once you've done your part of the process, you can hand it off to the person in your office who does the next task associated with the process. This saves you a lot of time, and you don't have to worry if your clients are being called enough or if you're discussing their most important issues with them. No more midnight wakeup sweats, worrying, "Oh my gosh, it's been way too long since I talked to Mrs. So-and-so," or "I haven't even seen Tom lately. I better reach out to him." When you schedule and document calls in your system, you know *exactly* how long it's been since you reached out to Tom. Automating your call cycles also allows you to scale, which we'll discuss more in the next section.

If you have the resources, line up your entire lead management system from initial contact by phone, web, email, or an event, through customer management. You can buy software that does this for you or hire a third party to help set it up, but *make sure it does what you want it to do for your team and your clients.* (I speak from experience: after spending several years building a system from scratch that didn't do what I needed it to do, I ended up scrapping it for a premade version that integrated with the business and delivered the results I wanted!)

Create a system and processes for your events, too. When I was working for a big financial firm and decided to do events, everyone told me they were a waste of time. But I knew my strengths, and I believed that I could do events well. I created processes around them, executed those processes, and looked at the results. Only one person showed up the first time; at the second event, there were four. Every event was another test and another opportunity to refine and improve my processes, and eventually I turned them into huge successes. I had built a complete, documented system that facilitated a complicated project, delivered great results every time, and was easily repeatable and scalable. When I started my own practice, I used this system for my town halls. If I ever sell the business, I can hand these events off to the new owner knowing they'll continue seamlessly. Another example is our client relationship management system—the Freedom Street Contact Management System—and the workflow within it. The system was inspired by a system developed by Brian Elms, a good friend and excellent advisor who's created a smart, purposeful communication cycle.

Instituting processes can be challenging for advisors stuck in a transaction-based model who depend on those transactions to get paid. Moving to a service-based model with the goal of creating long-term relationships helps with financial planning and outsider advisor relationships, and always being the fiduciary and putting the client first creates a more sustainable business model. Still, if you're stuck in a transaction model, look for where you can create repeatable processes.

Once you have your processes for all your activities in place, schedule them on a calendar so you're doing them at regular intervals. On my calendar, we complete three call cycles a year related to three major factors for our clients: income, performance, and risk. We have a minimum of two town halls every year where we educate the community with market updates and other issues of mass appeal. Twice a year, we do client appreciation events: an outdoor barbecue at the start of summer, and an indoor holiday open house in winter. These client events give us a chance to see our clients, and for them to see us, outside of the typical advisor-client relationship.

Advisors often put off process-building until later in their careers, but you can start creating them immediately. Begin every client relationship with the mindset that you'll be that person's advisor forever. View each one as a long-term relationship deserving of consistency, no matter how many more clients you take on or how busy you get. The only way you will accomplish this task is with repeatable processes that you use every day and can pass on years from now within your continuity plan. They will make your business more marketable, which is going to be very important to you down the road, or immediately, depending on your "next stage" timeline.

Scalability

Scaling your business is about taking on more of the right clients: replicating your best relationships and right-sizing your book of business to produce more, while minimizing the additional work involved. If it takes a certain number of hours to produce a particular amount of money, scaling allows you to double that amount of money without doubling your hours. This is what's referred to as "economies of scale," and you don't have to be a big corporation to realize the benefits of scaling. But what I found was, until I put the right team in place, scalability was only a dream and not something I could attain on my own.

Don't shy away from scaling your business. Think about it like this: People are often fearful of doing something they've never done. Once they've accomplished something new, they don't realize they can do the same thing at a much higher level. It's like the difference between swimming in a pool, swimming in a lake, and swimming in the ocean. No matter how big the body of water, you're still just swimming. Creating a scalable business allows you to advance from the pool to the ocean with minimal effort.

Instituting processes in your business frees you from a lot of work and a lot of worry, so you can scale effortlessly. Advisors who don't have processes aren't enjoying how they spend their time, and they aren't delivering the level of service their clients deserve. You can't properly deliver if you're not energized, organized, and methodical in your practices. Building a business that scales will get you there and put more money in your pocket.

Compliance

In this industry, playing by the rules and doing the right thing is mandatory regardless of who you work for. If you're at one of the larger firms, the company has people in place to ensure compliance. If you're an independent advisor or in the RIA channel, depending on your affiliation, that responsibility could be all yours. Delivering compliance accurately and consistently, no matter how big your business gets, is crucial. Take ownership of compliance, wherever you work. It's your responsibility to the business, and as an independent, to your team and your clients.

There's an old saying that goes something like this: "If a choice you made ended up on the front page of the newspaper and your mother read it, would she be proud of you?" If the answer is yes, then you made the right choice. If no, well then...you may have some soul-searching to do. Take the same approach with compliance.

Time management, processes, scalability, and compliance: take a hard look at how you manage them; then make a concerted effort to get them under control. Initially, this might require putting in extra time every day, but the results will be more time for you and a better experience for your clients and your team.

YOUR PEOPLE

A big part of running your business effectively is having the right people on your team. You're only as good as your partners—those other arms and legs and brains in the office.

I was always blessed to have a couple of full-time people who were awesome advisors and assistants. That doesn't mean they were always the best people *for me*. Early in my career, I needed to hire people to do more of what I did. As the business grew, I needed people who complemented my skills and could fill my blind spots.

I was lucky to find the perfect assistant to help me get the business off the ground. Amanda and I worked tirelessly, calling clients and developing a solid client base of great people and strong relationships. But eventually, we began to realize that our common strengths would only carry us so far. Along with those strengths, we also shared the same blind spots. I needed people to do what she and I could not do or did not have time for, so we built the team around that knowledge. Understanding those very blind spots allowed us to hire the right people to fill in the gaps.

I learned to be honest with myself and with others about my strengths and what I needed in my office to balance those out. This is harder than it sounds, because you're going to interview amazing people with whom you click immediately. Of course, if you're clicking because you share all of the same strengths, they'll be fun to have around the office, but you won't be serving your clients the way they deserve. You might have to make some tough decisions about your team, but you will be doing them and your clients a favor by building a team that will sustain you as your business grows.

Once you have the right people, you have to work toward the perfect balance. I was coaching an advisor whose new assistant, a young man, loved taking things off her plate—sometimes, all of her calls. This was to get the advisor out of "firefighter mode," which was great—at first. She soon discovered the assistant was taking *all* the calls and managing them, too, to the point that she didn't even know who was trying to reach her. There were people she wanted to speak with, or at least know they had called her so she could return their calls. She related a typical conversation to me:

"Who called while I was at lunch?" she'd ask.

"Oh, just Mrs. Johnson," replied the assistant.

"Why did she call?"

"Well, she said she was worried about the markets, but it wasn't a big deal and you don't need to call her back."

If Mrs. Johnson was worried about the markets, she definitely wanted to call her back. So while that assistant managed all those tasks that he believed the advisor wouldn't *want* to do, she had to have a conversation with him about her strengths and where they superseded his—such as knowing whether a client needed to be called back. As you grow your team, all these issues happen early and often. But you get better. And in time, you can reach a happy medium by understanding one another's personalities, strengths, and weaknesses, and building working relationships around them.

LAYING THE GROUNDWORK FOR A BETTER TOMORROW

There's an added bonus to all this work, because tackling these obstacles will help you both today and tomorrow. In other words, running your business effectively enhances your productivity and wealth now, and it will also put you and your business in a better position for your eventual exit, whether that be selling the business, merging with another team, or merely setting up a continuity plan for succession.

YOUR NEXT STAGE TERMINOLOGY

Your next stage can take several forms. To avoid confusion, here are the terms that I use to define that next stage and what they mean:

Acquisition is selling your business. You might begin by partnering with a company, and then selling your book of business to them.

Succession is creating a continuity plan that keeps your business running after you leave it, to set up an eventual sale.

Affiliation refers to aligning your business with another company—merging or sharing resources.

Advisors want a rich life, while at the same time, they want to make sure they're taking the right steps to ensure their business has value when the time comes for them to exit the company. They want to ensure their plan makes sense and is executed properly.

We've all read stories about celebrities who passed away with no plans in place for their businesses. Their multimillion-dollar estates end up in disarray, and their families, employees, and business partners are left to pick up the pieces. No doubt, you have discussions with your clients about what happens to their estates in the future. You might have a plan for your own family, but what about your business?

Look back on your career, all the hard work and sacrifices to build your business and your wealth. All those people—your family, employees, partners, and of course, your clients—depend on you. If you value those people, you need a continuity plan. An intentional, marketable plan for your business's future is imperative for creating your rich life today. Even if your eventual departure date is decades in the future, laying the groundwork now will put your mind at ease. You'll be able to focus on the here and now, slowly putting the pieces together for your future, instead of worrying about it or denying that time will ever come.

I've seen advisors struggle with a lot of issues, and I've dealt with many of those same challenges myself. Through introspection and self-awareness—and by making a lot of mistakes, the old "trial and error" method—I've figured out which activities and people serve me and which do not. The next step for me was coming up with a plan to shift how I operated in this world.

In the next chapter, we'll talk about what you can do to focus more energy on what's working and stop wasting your time on what isn't, with the goal of creating a rich life.

CHAPTER ONE QUESTIONS

1. Do you see yourself in Hardworking Hank or Laid-Back Lonnie? Are you happy this way, or do you think there's a better way to live?

2. Do you feel like the only value you have to offer is how many hours you work or how much money you make? What else do you have to offer that people would value, and how would it feel if you allowed yourself the time to offer those talents and skills?

3. What's your life/work balance like? Honestly, think about how much time you devote to each. Are you satisfied with that balance? Where are you giving your love?

4. Can you ever really have life/work balance? Are you self-aware enough to identify temporary imbalances so you know when to adjust?

5. Do you think about the value of your business now and in the future, when you might want to sell it? What are you doing today to make it valuable to another advisor or firm? Do you know what your business is worth? What are your current options with your employer, company, or platform?

CHAPTER 2

What Matters Most

*There's nowhere you can be
that isn't where you're meant to be.*
—John Lennon

What I love most about this business is the same today as when I started. It was never about the cold calls, the appointments, or even the sales, and it certainly was never about the market and its fluctuations. I love dealing with clients—always have. And I love mentoring other advisors. I love being there for people when they need me and helping them solve their problems. When I can't solve their problems, I connect them with someone who can. Whether it's a paralegal, a contractor, or a wedding planner, I have a knack for being the networking hub who brings people together, and I love how this profession supports that.

In any job, you're often asked if you want to give back in some capacity beyond your role or job description. When asked, I've always said yes. I see helping out as a chance to learn and develop as a person. Before going independent, I worked at another firm where I did a *whole lot* of learning and developing. My "giving back" work was usually coaching new advisors. It didn't contribute directly to my bottom line financially, but it made me better at everything I did in my job, and I loved every minute of it. When I helped people, it didn't feel like work. Coaching a new advisor on their phone skills didn't take away from my success—it made me feel even more powerful, especially when they succeeded. This is a part of who I am and who I've always been. I light up when I can help people maximize their own human potential. Filling my dual roles as advisor and advisor coach was a balancing act, but I loved the challenge.

Aside from the personal payoff of helping other advisors and my clients solve their problems, I could see that the financial payoff would allow me to take care of my family the way I wanted at the time, and in the future. The only downside of that role was the constant prospecting, a task I never truly enjoyed. Mentoring advisors, on the other hand, was all about helping people solve their problems and reach their potential. There was never a shortage of advisors who needed my help, so no "prospecting" was required. Because I enjoyed it so much and the company enjoyed having me do it, I ended up spending a large chunk of my time training people. Even though the situation wasn't ideal financially, I was discovering what I loved doing, was really good at, and made me feel fulfilled.

I told you in the introduction that I would be sharing stories with you and that some of them were personal. One of those stories is from many years ago, and while it has nothing to do with financial freedom, the experience had a dramatic effect on me. To this day, I believe it's where my drive to live my own legacy by keeping others safe however I can—in my life, my business, and through my charitable work—comes from.

One night when I was about three years old, I heard a noise and got out of bed to investigate. My parents were on a date, and so I assumed they had come home early and that the man in the kitchen was my dad. I watched as he pulled a big knife from a drawer.

"Dad?" I called out. But when the man turned around, I saw it was a stranger. He chased me into my room, and then he was gone. I found my little kid's bat and went after him. To my horror, he was in the living room, assaulting my babysitter. I swung at him as hard as I could, but he just chased me back into my room.

This time, I slammed the door behind me and put a chair against it, like I'd seen in cartoons.

I thank God every day that I don't remember everything that happened that night. What I do remember is the police coming. My parents were there too. Somebody wrapped me in a blanket and the police asked me a lot of questions. I told them everything I saw, and based on my description of the intruder, they caught him.

I was probably traumatized, but I honestly do not remember. I do remember how it felt to want to help that girl, and I remember how it felt when they caught her attacker.

That desire to protect others never went away, not entirely. Before getting into finance, I wanted to be a police officer or an FBI agent. They had all been so calm and in control that night. And I wanted to use the skills I'd developed from that experience—the toughness, the resilience—to keep myself and my family safe. On sleepless nights, and in times of fear, I had learned how to calm my brain by planning my actions and with deep breathing and self-talk, such as "What happened is so rare, so random, and will never likely happen again. But if it does, what will you do? What are your escape routes?"

Two major takeaways that I'm especially grateful for are that my mom did talk about what happened and encouraged me to talk about it. My parents didn't make me feel weird or different, and they didn't make me go to some kid counselor. Maybe if they had, I would have gotten over it faster and in a different way, but I don't think I would have developed the resilience that came with dealing with it in my own way.

Looking back on the experiences that defined who I would become as an adult and ultimately drive my legacy, that night was one of the most impactful of my childhood. It instilled in me a need to protect people, to stay calm no matter what happened, and to always be looking for a way out. This passion shows itself in the work I do for my clients. It's in the training I provide other advisors and in how I treat people in our business. It's one of the main reasons I'm drawn to working alongside women and serving them as clients, and why it's so important to me that they know that when they talk to me, they are heard. It's a powerful force behind why I am so engaged in working with people who are looking for the next stage in their careers and aren't quite sure where to turn or what to do. The circumstances are much different and the consequences and potential outcomes may not be as dire as what I experienced years ago, but I will always have that need to do what I can to help people take that next step toward safety.

FINDING WHAT MATTERS IN THE WORK

Think about the life cycle of a financial advisor. You start out like a hustler or a peddler, telling everyone and anyone who will listen what you can do for them, and praying that they'll give you a shot. Then you become a salesperson and you go through a phase where you've successfully figured out how to get people in the room and sell your services. *Selling services* is more like selling yourself and your advice—not products. You learn to move to the next step properly, and then you become a financial consultant. Clients rely on you for their financial needs, but the conversations still revolve around money. Finally, if you do everything right, a transformation occurs and you become an actual advisor.

FOR THE ADVISOR,
THE FINANCIAL INDUSTRY HAS MATURED

The industry has grown up so much from where it was when I started. Two decades have led to a mainly college-educated field with many new and important designations that round out practices for the better and serve the client deeper. From the CFP to the ChFC and many more professional designations today, advisors are given a great path to learn more and grow in the profession. Proper training and better regulation have shifted the old sales model to that of one based on service and fiduciary standards. True servant leadership is the way the industry has shifted and even the old "salesy" investment reps have shifted to the new world.

The *title* "financial advisor" doesn't put you in that advisor role. It's something you earn over time, as you understand your clients and prove your trustworthiness to them to the extent that they come to you for much more than money advice. You are their life advisor on many levels, helping them make decisions about everything from family to vacations and liabilities to insurance. You are referring them to your friends, and they're referring their friends to you. You get very close to these people, and your lives are better for it. That's the major payoff of growing into a true, trusted advisor.

Looking back at the Monday, Tuesday, Wednesday, etc. advisors, you can clearly see how the natural progression from hustler to salesperson to advisor evolves for people who stay with it, care enough, and are skilled enough to do it well. And along the way, if you're paying attention, you begin to find out what matters to you.

Following My Heart

That's how it was for me. Over time, as I became more aware of what mattered and what I enjoyed, I also became aware that I was outgrowing my position at the firm. Don't get me wrong—I learned a lot in that position. They had a process that worked: (1) Talk to twenty-five people a day; (2) ask open-ended questions to understand their financial needs; (3) present an appropriate solution; (4) assess and document the contact; and (5) indicate the next action. As I advanced in my role as both an advisor and a trainer of new advisors, I took on more responsibilities and kept getting promoted until I was leading recruiting. I always pushed to get ahead, but in hindsight I can see that I wasn't the best strategist when it came to my own career. To move through the ranks at a large firm, there's politics and gamesmanship—certain boxes need to be checked. I could see how the game was played, but playing it just wasn't me and that probably held me back. Seeing the people I worked with become fully trained and successful was more important than leaving them behind while I moved on. I probably stayed in each position a bit longer than I should have, but my focus was really on helping the people I trained. I loved seeing their growth and success and frankly, wasn't worried about checking boxes. Perhaps I should have been more selfish, but the experience was a good lesson for me.

When I was ready, I took a senior role in performance, which involved advisor development and managing other leaders on our team as well as the coordination of training for the region on growth and business development. If people weren't hitting their numbers, I worked with them to make sure they did. Eventually, I was in a management role and focused heavily on the operations—basically, I was the chief operating officer for the region. The next rung on the ladder would be regional manager, and everyone told me I was in a great position for the job.

They were right: the company was conducting informal interviews with me and a couple of other candidates. I became keenly aware of how my dedication to other advisors might hurt me. The management mentality is to grind away, always reaching for that next rung. That wasn't my priority—helping people was. Helping people *always* was. I wanted to leave each person I worked with fully prepared for the next step, and I wanted to leave each position fully developed for the next person who stepped into the role. I wanted to make a positive impact and leave a legacy that would last beyond my time at the job: true leadership development.

Finally, it was down to me and one other candidate. People who knew me said I was a slam dunk for the position, but in my mind the other guy was a better fit for the company. He was older, more seasoned, and had previous management experience as a military officer. Win or lose, I had done the job the way I thought it should be done, or at least how it made sense to me, by taking care of the people and the business and not worrying so much about how quickly I was promoted. Ultimately, we all wanted the best for our clients, fellow advisors, and the leadership team, and that's what I focused on.

A Temporary Letdown

Well, in a popular vote I probably would have been "elected." But I didn't win the electoral college, and I didn't get the job. At first, the news was devastating. Here I was, after spending more than a decade making our region the best, doing everything I could to improve the whole company. It seemed that every concept, every idea, every project and program I'd started and shared freely with anyone who needed it didn't count for anything. I felt like it had all been for nothing, because in the end, I wasn't the person they wanted in that role. I learned something about myself in the weeks that followed, and I had time to reflect: I valued leadership, but I didn't enjoy management. Missing out on that opportunity stung, but the more I thought about it, the more I agreed with the decision.

To put it into perspective, I thought about the time when I got a job mowing lawns as a kid. I didn't just cut the grass—I edged the lawn, pulled the weeds, and cleaned up all the trimmings. I ended up with the same five bucks I would've gotten for just mowing the lawn. Thinking about that made me question if I was a fool for doing not only what was asked of me but doing my best. Of course, I wasn't a fool at all. But losing was painful. I've always preferred winning. Like author John Maxwell says, "Sometimes you win, sometimes you learn." I was learning all right!

After hearing I didn't get the job, I drove home from work feeling a bit empty. Had I just wasted all those years? *No*, I thought. *I learned and I grew, and I'm going to figure out what makes sense next.* Still, telling my wife was painful. Even though I knew I had done my best, I still felt like sort of a failure.

That night, instead of dwelling on the situation, I focused on what was important: I checked in on my youngest son, who was fast asleep. Then I checked on my older boy, who was still awake. I lied down next to him in bed, and we talked for a while, and I started feeling a little better. Then I went downstairs, and my wife took my hand and led me into the backyard. "Let's go swimming," she said, and slipped off her robe. *What's going on?* I wondered; *she never wants to swim—especially at night!* Then she popped open a bottle of champagne and poured out two glasses.

I was, in a word, shocked. I had come home with the worst news ever—or so I thought—and here was my gorgeous wife in her birthday suit, handing me a glass of bubbly. *JACKPOT!*

"I know you're disappointed about the job," she said, "and you're not going to like what I have to say. But this is the best thing that could have happened. It's not the right role for you. It's not who you are. You would have been unhappy, and that job would have taken you away from me and the kids. I want you to do what makes you happy and brings us together."

There it was. My wife had just said out loud what I was afraid to ask myself: What was I worth to the people who mattered most? A title? A position? More money? No, not to the people I cared for the most. Those people—my family—wanted me to be happy. And they wanted more of *me*.

I suspected my clients and the advisors I trained felt the same, but they weren't calling the shots. Still, it felt good to hear those words—like doing what I believed in was going to work out for the best somehow. In the back of my mind, I knew that all the extra effort I had put into my roles at the company weren't for nothing, because I would use them in a future role that I just hadn't figured out yet.

I humbled myself and went back to my role working for the new regional manager—the guy I had lost the job to. I could have quit, but I liked the guy and had a lot of respect for him. His success was important to me, and besides, I wanted to stay around awhile and make sure I was leaving my position in the best state for whoever filled it next.

Around this time, I knew that at some point I had to start my own business. I needed a company that I could run the way I wanted to run it. I had been preparing for this moment for years—studying what I did, researching other companies and their methods, and thinking about how I would do things differently. Even though there was much more to learn, I was ready and willing. The time was right to move on. The key for me was building on my strengths:

splitting my time between coaching advisors and providing my clients with top-level service.

It was the kind of work that made me light up. It also helped me realize that by running my own business, I could do more of it and hire other people to do everything else. And most importantly, I'd be able to do it right—by putting the people first. I wouldn't have to wear myself out for another company to do it.

TIME TO REFLECT

I'm so thankful I didn't get that job. I didn't realize it in the moment (even though my wife did), but it was the best possible outcome. I had been running myself ragged for another company, other people, and for what? To feel more important? Have more status within the company? Did I need more words of affirmation? It might have been a little bit of all of those things for me in the beginning. I was also searching for whatever I could do really well. I was finding my niche. I loved working with people, and I enjoyed the business aspect, too—how to improve each role, each department, and each person I was involved with in my climb up the corporate ladder. That's what lit me up.

In the months that followed, I had time to reflect on what had kept me there for so long. It wasn't the day-to-day company BS that wasted everyone's time, that's for sure. It was the people and the culture.

Our regional meetings, for example, were so wonderfully family oriented that my wife and kids actually looked forward to them every year. Around the meetings, there were lots of activities to enjoy with all the other advisors and their families too. You really felt like you were all part of one big family. On top of that, we had two trips a year, and they'd set us up at five-star resorts. Because of the size of the business, they'd get great discounts and could afford to send us to these places, and all we had to pay were the taxes. These weren't forced vacations, and we had the option of skipping them to work or take paid vacation time, but I never did. The life/work combination—traveling with friends from work, getting to know their families, and being able to mix business with a great vacation—gave my family some of our best memories. We developed real relationships and for a while, lasting friendships. As amazing as the culture was, though, something was pushing me to move on.

I had been making a difference over the years, and every time I saw the positive effect, I wanted to do more. But no matter how much I did, it would never be enough. Many companies, and people in companies, are wired to demand more, more, more from their people, and employees knock themselves out to meet the demands. In the end, you have to ask yourself: What am I doing this for? What am I working for? If the goal is to satisfy the employer, you can never do enough for that to happen.

This isn't just corporate culture—I think it's also part of human nature. I began to see this demand for more, more, more when I started my own business and got sucked into the same mentality. The team that handles our company newsletter does an amazing job, yet I am always looking for ways for them to improve it because that's part of who I am. Yet, to the team, it probably sounds like I am always demanding more. "Make it repeatable. Make it scalable. Document the process," I say. Kind of what I used to hear about my own work at the previous company! Amazing, right, how switching seats can open your eyes to a new perspective and allow you to see things from a different point of view?

I have to consciously hold back at times and remember to let them know how terrific their work is, and that it's fine just as it is. Then I can offer some feedback on what they could do different the next time. It's important to me that people understand how I fully appreciate everything they've done, because I remember what it feels like when a company is always asking for more, as if I have not already done enough.

Reflecting on what I did right and what I did wrong earlier in my career guided me in my own practice, but I still made mistakes, and continue to make them even today. And I continue to reflect, learn, and grow.

THE PARETO PRINCIPLE

I'm sure you've heard of the Pareto Principle or "80/20 Rule," which states, "80 percent of consequences come from 20 percent of the causes, asserting an unequal relationship between inputs and outputs."[1] Simply put, your 20 percent counts for a lot more than your 80 percent.

---

1 Jim Chappelow (reviewer), "Pareto Principle," *Investopedia*, updated August 29, 2019, https://www.investopedia.com/terms/p/paretoprinciple.asp.

All through my career, I've lived by this principle, asking myself *Where does 80 percent of my time go? Are the top 20 percent of my clients getting the attention they need and deserve?* I've even broken down the top 20 percent of activities that make up my work and the top 20 percent of my clients into 20 percent and 80 percent segments, to figure out if I'm spending enough time on what and who needs the most attention. And remember, I'm not the analytical one in my office!

Remember Hardworking Hank, who gave all his time and his love to his practice? This left very little for anything or anyone else. Where you invest your love, you invest your time, and where you invest your time, you invest your love. However, when we do this automatically, without actually thinking about it, we can end up investing all our time into people and work that we don't love. Think about it: Do you love the people you spend the most time with? And what about the people you love the most—how much time do they get with you? What about your job? Do you love what you do, or do you spend most of your workday doing things you hate?

My goal was to spend 20 percent of my time doing what I had to and being disciplined enough about it to make it count. That left 80 percent of my time to do what I loved doing, with people I enjoyed being around. For that to happen, I would have to make some serious changes in my life. First, I needed to get to know myself a little better.

WHO ARE YOU?

Self-awareness is one of the greatest tools that anyone can have in business and in life. Understanding what you're great at and not so great at, who you are and who you aren't is powerful information. I had experience with personality assessments—taking them myself and using them to help my leadership team—and was impressed by the results. Wanting to learn more, I took a deep dive with formal training and got certified so I could teach assessments like DiSC (Dominant, Inspiring, Supportive, and Cautious) to others. The self-evaluation models of human behavior taught me about myself and helped explain why I worked better with certain team members than with others. I had known this but hadn't really been utilizing the information. The training reminded me how people's different personalities can complement each other for synergy, teamwork, and a more productive working relationship.

With this new understanding of my personality and strengths, I looked at what I had been doing at the company I had just left. I didn't just look at it—I wrote it down. I wanted to know exactly how I had been spending my time. Well, more than 80 percent of the time, I discovered, was spent doing stuff I didn't enjoy. The stuff I really loved and was good at accounted for less than 20 percent of my workday. So I set out a new goal for my role in my new business: revisit my assessments, consciously identify my greatest strengths, and build my career around them.

Don't confuse what you *can* do with what you *want* to do. I can do many things well, and some things much better than other advisors I've worked with, but that doesn't mean I enjoy doing them. So I had to think about that, too: *What am I doing that makes me look good because I do it well, but that I dread doing?*

Early in my career, I knew I didn't like cold calling. I hated making phone calls and knocking on doors, because I didn't feel like it was the best way to help people who needed and wanted what I had to offer.

I loved doing events, and had no problem calling people to invite them to a seminar. I never talked about our company at these events. They were education-focused, and there was no selling at all. Instead, the conversations were about the people who showed up and what I could teach them about topics like managing retirement income. This was when baby boomers were getting to retirement age, and the market was down. There was a lot of fear and uncertainty, and I felt that educating the community on the subject was a worthwhile use of my time.

I didn't just wing it when it came to events. Every seminar was planned and scheduled to the most minor detail, from where each person sat, to the timing of the salad, drink refills, and dessert. I documented the process and refined it so every event went like clockwork.

At first, I was hand-signing every invitation because I thought the personal touch would be important to people. One time I forgot to sign them, and we had the same response as with the signed ones, so I stopped doing it after that. I hired a third party to send 1,500 mailers for me. We followed up the mailers with phone calls to gauge people's interest and encourage them to attend. These events were held at a restaurant and everyone had dinner, but I would negotiate a lunch rate with the restaurant because most of the people were older and they didn't want a huge meal. A six-ounce fillet, rather than a twelve-ounce T-bone, along with all the salad and side dishes, was plenty. This saved me a lot of money, while still giving everyone a good experience. I thought that if I helped people understand their options and opportunities over a nice meal at a free seminar, they would look to me when the time was right for them to make a decision about their finances.

These were educational, and I was providing a needed service without assuming that every attendee would hire me. There was no pressure on the people who showed up, and no pressure on me to make them clients. If enough people showed up, I'd get a certain number of appointments and a certain number of those appointments would turn into new clients. This was how I built my pipeline by doing what I was very good at *and* enjoyed.

Within a few years, I was so busy with all the referrals I was getting, servicing my client base, and doing more for my community, that I stopped doing seminars and began holding town halls with my existing client base and their friends. This way, I could speak with many interested people in-depth, at one time, on topics that concerned many of them. Some months, one hundred people would show up, and other times I'd have an audience of a dozen or so people. But I was consistent about the town halls. I wanted my clients to know that no matter what happened or how bad the market got—and it got pretty bad for a few years—I was still there and not hiding in my office, and still willing to answer questions and talk about it.

A side effect of these town halls was that I got fewer calls from people worried about the market. They were getting enough information from me at these group talks, and they were seeing that other people were in similar situations as them. This helped calm people, I think, and the reactive calls that I would usually get decreased.

Early in my career, I also discovered that I did not like selling people anything without knowing their story first. I didn't enjoy completing transactions for people just to make a buck in early cold calling sessions. I'd be in the middle of selling a stock or a bond to a person, and I'd want to know more: Why did they want to buy it? What were they going to do with it, and what were their plans for the future? I'd literally say to a client, "I can put that order in today, but I would really love to set up an appointment, so I could make sure that this is appropriate for you and in your best interest." This was how I had to do business. It made sense, and I felt good about it. It was the right approach for me and for the client.

Equally important to doing what you love is surrounding yourself with the people you enjoy most. Can you imagine spending 80 percent of your workday doing what you love and excel at, with people you really want to be around? You can do that. Consider your own personality, your strengths, and your weaknesses.

What do you like to do and do well? Who are the people that will complement that work with their own unique skills and talents? Are you outgoing? Do you like to be the rainmaker in the business? Do you want to talk to clients all the time? If this is you, you need a person on your team to take care of other types of tasks, like the financial plans within the practice. Looking ahead, you may want to merge with an individual or a company that's very good at what you are not, or what you simply don't want to do.

This comes down to drive—what drives you. It's not motivation, which is fleeting and dies quickly. You're motivated to do something and once it's accomplished, you move on. Drive has depth and passion behind it. Have you ever listened to a motivational speaker and then gone on to achieve something? How long did that feeling last before it burned out and you went back to doing whatever you usually do? This, by the way, is why I would not want to be a "motivational speaker." I'd rather be a change agent—a person who creates rippling effects that change a person's life in the moment and forever. I want you to really think about who you are and what makes you happy.

Figuring out what makes you happy can be harder than it sounds. You can get lost in the company you're at and the company you keep. I did. For years, I told myself I loved what I was doing, but in truth, I was really starting to resent it. Being productive feels good, but it's temporary and shallow if you're not happy in the moment, doing what you love with people you enjoy.

E.L.F.® VS. H.A.L.F.™

I believe in surrounding myself with people who outproduce me, have bigger businesses than I do, and whose accomplishments I admire. I learn from them. Similarly, I seek out mentors outside the industry. Financial advisors can get lost in the business and forget there's a whole world out there from which to learn.

Author and marketing executive Joe Polish runs a group called Genius Network, where business leaders share their insights about business and life. The fundamental basis for everything Joe teaches is E.L.F.: *easy, lucrative, and fun,* which he recommends applying to help you decide how you feel about what you do at work and in the rest of your life. The goal is to find out if they're easy, lucrative, and fun—or if they're *hard, annoying, lame, and frustrating* (H.A.L.F.). In Joe's exercise, you write everything you do in a two-column list, with the E.L.F. work in the A column and everything else in the B column.

Column A will show you what you truly enjoy and are probably really good at. It's the work that makes you money, too, and you should be doing more of it and less of all that other stuff. Beyond the work, E.L.F. also works for evaluating your relationships. Think about the people you deal with on a day-to-day basis. If you get the butterflies in your stomach (the bad "I think I'm going to throw up" kind, not the good "I think I'm in love" kind) every time a certain client calls, stop serving them. Literally fire them as clients. We advisors think we have to serve everyone who needs our help, especially lucrative clients, but we don't. Clients like those suck the life out of you, and then you have nothing left to give the clients who are easy, lucrative, and fun. Liberate yourself from the H.A.L.F. people in your life—you and your time are too valuable to waste on them. Commit yourself to those clients who make you happy instead.

When I did this exercise, my E.L.F. column included doing events and town halls, client relationships, collaborating with the people on my team, and working on business growth. I added public speaking, exercise, and time with my family. It was clear to me how I should be spending at least 80 percent of my time, and where I should be committing 80 percent of my love.

In my B column were activities that weren't easy, lucrative, or fun. I didn't want to give all of them up, though. I thought that if I could figure out a different way to do them, I could move them to the A column. One example is my participation in the Boys and Girls Club. I'm on the board, but I didn't feel like I was making enough of an impact to warrant the time and effort I put into the group. Instead, I worked on building membership for a year, and getting people to assume roles on smaller unit boards so I could then step away from the day-to-day operations and focus on consulting for the larger regional corporate board. That change made me feel comfortable moving my involvement in the club to the A column because I enjoyed it.

THE HUMAN TOUCH

In your 20 percent and in your E.L.F. columns, don't neglect those activities that involve connecting with people. I don't mean making small talk or having scripted conversations, but looking people in the eye and speaking with them. Ask people how they're doing. Listen for the answer. The people around you may be going through a lot but will never let you know unless you ask.

I once received a client from an advisor who seemed only too happy to be passing her on. His advice to me was, "Just let her talk herself out, and then you can tell her what you need to do." His comment gave me pause. I went to see the client, a woman in her mid-70s, uncertain about what to expect. The woman, who was retired and had $7 million with our company, told me that she was ready to take her business to another firm because she did not like the advisor she'd been working with—the guy who had given me that odd advice.

I spent four hours at her house. We shared a glass of wine and talked about our families, and I got to know this wonderful woman very well. It was a great way to spend an afternoon, and she became one of my favorite clients. In the end, whether the market goes up or down, we still have that relationship because it's built on a real connection of human touch, not on market performance. That advisor back at the office, with his brusque attitude, missed out on all of that.

I had another client whose company I enjoyed so much, I would schedule our visits for the end of the day, so we could enjoy a cup of coffee together and talk about our families and our lives. She was my client and my friend for eighteen years when she passed away. I spoke with her grandson at the funeral, and he expressed his gratitude for the friendship I had shared with this woman, his grandmother. If you're looking for a payoff for building these kinds of relationships, you're in it for the wrong reason. Stop thinking about the business, enjoy the people, and the people will want to do business with you. And your work won't feel like work anymore. You might actually begin to love it.

This is how you make your identity more than just your job. If all you are to another person is someone who takes care of their finances, the two of you do not have a relationship. Working that way will come back to haunt you when you exit the business, because you will have built nothing. Your clients won't miss you, because they never knew you. And they won't stay in touch with you or invite you to their parties and family functions, because you were never that close. Don't pass up all those opportunities to make real connections.

If you struggle with creating these relationships, you're not alone. We tend to get inside our own heads, focused on our own goals, and we're oblivious to everything that doesn't "fit" that focus. Add to that the convenience of a smartphone and social media—human interaction is a tap or a swipe away, so it's easier to stare at our phones than to look at the person in front of us. When's the last time you struck up a conversation with a person in line at the grocery store or in the waiting room at the dentist's office? Step into an elevator and see how quick people are to pull out their phones to manage the awkwardness. It's almost like a defense mechanism. Unfortunately, it's who we've become. I sometimes do it, too, and I'm not proud to admit it. But I'm well aware—and always working on it.

The second reason we avoid these relationships is time. When you're so busy that you can't breathe, you don't notice other people. You don't respond to human interaction because you're always on a deadline and you've hardened yourself to anything that might distract you from that deadline. I'm guilty of this as well, but when I recognize it, I remind myself that as important as it is for me to have a schedule and maintain the discipline to follow it, my life is worth nothing if I can't take the time for people.

A client once told me that a person's business can be their ministry. I believe that. If you care enough about your clients to build those strong relationships and give them more of yourself than what's required in your financial advisor role, you are in a sense building a ministry. So, when you're thinking about your 20 percent, consider the relationships you have and how they make you feel. Ask yourself how you can make them better by focusing on that human touch, instead of on your short-term objectives. Give people the gift of your attention. What you receive in return—beyond the business and the money—is much more than you can imagine.

YOU CAN LIE TO ME,
BUT YOU CANNOT LIE TO YOURSELF

It's easy to get into the habit of saying out loud and to yourself what you want to be true, even if it isn't. When you repeat these "beliefs" often enough, you start to believe them. How many times have you heard someone say, "I love my job"? Yet, they dread going to work, seem miserable the whole day, and can't wait to get out of there at five o'clock. That doesn't sound like someone who loves what they do.

Or they convince themselves that they're doing a great job at work, when in reality, they barely show up. These are the advisors who brag about their terrific life/work balance—because they spend so much time at home—but who are outwardly upset when they miss out on true financial freedom. On the other side of the coin are people who give everything to the job and will tell you their lives are peachy, but they're falling apart.

None of us is perfect, and I admit that I've lied to myself on occasion. Like when I come home a little late after a very long day, and I'm in a snippy mood. Being aware of this and wanting to be better for my family makes me stop and think before I walk through the door. I might take a few deep breaths to reset my mood. Sometimes this works, but not always—I'm a work in progress. But I can't work all day and then come home on empty—my family deserves better than that. I need to leave something in the tank for those precious hours at home, and I need to be honest with myself about just how important it is that I show up with the right energy and mindset for the people I care about most.

You might say you love your job, and you probably love something about your job, but if there are parts you don't love, be honest with yourself about it. Do you love maintaining a six-appointments-a-day schedule, eating at your desk or in your car, and focusing all your conversations on long-term care, annuities, and investment performance, without actually seeing your clients as people with lives, loves, problems, and interests beyond their finances? I don't know any advisors who would love that job, yet many of them do exactly that, day in and day out. That's not why I got into this business, and I doubt if it was your goal. Happiness is a choice; joy is awareness of the daily moments that bring us a smile. Often, we become numb to those moments. You can tell yourself you're happy, and tell anyone else within earshot that you're happy, but are you really? I had to answer that question for myself, and then I had to do something about it, to create a rich life. Because freedom is not about denial. It's about being honest with yourself about a life that fulfills you, and then making that life your reality.

CHAPTER TWO QUESTIONS

1. What lights you up? What are you giving 20 percent to that you would prefer to give 80 percent?

2. How much time do you spend doing those things?

3. How much time do you spend with your favorite people?

4. What can you do to change how you spend your time?

CHAPTER 3

Finding the Perfect Balance

The best and safest thing is to keep a balance in your life, ac-knowledge the great powers around us and in us. If you can do that, and live that way, you are really a wise man.
—Euripides

Ａs a young person, I saw my father get up every day at the same time, put on his uniform, and—lunch pail in hand—go to his job as a warehouse manager. For a period of time, we had only one car and my mother needed it for her job as a paralegal, so Dad rode his bicycle to work. He never missed a day.

My father valued loyalty and consistency: he got to work on time and was home by four o'clock. He earned a regular paycheck, and we had food on the table and a roof over our heads. Dad wanted to give us everything that he didn't have growing up—a certain predictability that made us feel loved. This, to him, was the epitome of success.

Mom and Dad were paid about the same, but she had to work more hours because of her salaried, rather than hourly, position. She handled most of the finances, squeezing every penny and negotiating payments when she had to. She never left a bill unpaid, no matter how tough times were. We weren't hurting financially, but we struggled at times, so I wondered why my father didn't find a job that valued him more—and paid more. I was too young to understand the balance my father was trying to maintain between making enough to pay the bills without sacrificing family time. It was nice to have him home early every day so I wouldn't have to be alone after school, but I never fully appreciated it. I'm ashamed to admit that now, especially being a father myself and understanding the value of spending time with my sons.

I always admired my father's unwavering commitment to provide for us, though. For that, he was my hero. And I admired my mother's diligence in honoring the family's debts. But I also knew that I wanted more. I wanted to someday be able to give my family everything, and help provide for my mother and father, too.

For a while, Dad took on a second job to help save money for that second car. One day he came home all excited. He had bought a brand-new Chevy truck with all the bells and whistles. My father was beaming at the dinner table, telling us all about the truck. My mother told my sister and me to leave the table and go to our rooms. We sat by the door, listening, and my mother really lit into Dad. Even with our father's second job, she was still working sixty, seventy hours a week to pay the bills, and driving a 1970s Maverick that was always breaking down. We piled into the Maverick and went to the Ford dealership where my parents spent what felt, to me, like ten hours dealing with the salesperson and the bank, finally trading in the Maverick and coming away with an Escort station wagon. Part of me felt so bad for my dad—he worked hard and deserved good things. Poor Dad had been so excited about that truck; he didn't want the wagon. Another part of me was confused, because he hadn't consulted my mom about such a huge purchase.

Mom drove the Escort to and from her job, and Dad had to keep riding the bike. I didn't understand why we couldn't have another good car, but I trusted my parents and believed they were making the best decisions for our family. At the same time, the experience was emotional and impactful. It stuck with me, and I decided that I never, ever wanted to be broke. I began to see money as freedom. Financial freedom could be a calming force, alleviating the pain around many of life's challenges. Even back then, my mind was working away, the wheels turning, trying to solve this problem of how to make our lives better. Financial freedom might not solve all our problems, but it would allow me to let go of the scarcity mindset that affects anyone who's struggled, and many who have not—the fear that the money could go away at any minute and with it, all options in life.

Even though my parents struggled financially at times, when it came to where they spent their money, my sister and I always came first. They sent us to Catholic school instead of public school. I didn't understand why at the time, but looking back, I'm thankful for my years at St. Gregory the Great Catholic School. The service mentality that I have today, I owe to my early education. My religion was always there for me during the hard times. Weekly mass, coupled with my Monday through Friday studies, formed the powerfully influential and positive backbone that empowered my confidence in the future.

Hindsight really is 20/20. My father knew that spending time with his kids was more important than making a few hundred more dollars. For him, a happy family life was more important than a new truck, and a good education was one of the best things he could offer his children. Through this older and somewhat wiser lens, I now know that my father was immensely successful.

We played a lot of basketball in those afternoons, and my father was pretty hard on me. We had similar personalities and were like oil and water when we got into it—he didn't want to listen to me, and I didn't want to listen to him either. But despite the challenges, I cherish those times because him just being present made a huge difference in my life. He set a standard, which is more than many of us offer the people with whom we interact every day.

As a husband, a father, and a business owner, being present can be a constant struggle. Advisors are always "on" because our clients need us at all hours of the day. Separating yourself from work and the rest of your life to focus on the person in front of you is difficult. My father had mastered that balance by giving his job so many hours, sticking to that schedule, and clocking out to spend the rest of his day with his family.

That kind of separation isn't so simple when clients are counting on you to respond to their needs. This is especially true in today's world of immediate gratification, when every voicemail left, every email and text message sent, expectantly awaits a response. And we *want* to respond. It's only human to feel personally responsible for clients. They count on us to get them through some of the toughest times. But to achieve balance in your life, you have to let go a little bit, commit to spending time on those other activities and people that matter, put them on your schedule, and have the discipline to stick to it.

You might think having that time isn't possible, but here again is where having systems and processes in place and the right people on your staff is so critical. You have every right to put your phone away during dinner, and after dinner when you're reading to your kids. It's not just a right, but a responsibility to yourself and your family. When you take a vacation, someone else should be in place to manage the business so you don't have to respond to every email, text, and phone call that comes in while you're on the beach, reading a book, or just enjoying the rare, uninterrupted company of your spouse. It all comes down to figuring out what matters to you, and making it a priority.

ROCKS, PEBBLES, AND SAND

Getting your head straight about what's important and what can wait is how you begin to prioritize. It's like the rocks, pebbles, and sand story about time management. If you don't put the big rocks in your jar of life first, and then top them off with pebbles and sand to filter down and fill the spaces, you'll never fit those rocks in there.

The rocks represent the most important priorities in your life. The pebbles and sand are less essential in the moment. It's important to identify your biggest priorities and think about how you may be avoiding them. Some of us are masters at avoidance. It's just a whole lot easier to spend time on the little stuff—playing in the sand. Sandboxes are for kids. Adults, it's time to get out of the sandbox!

Too often, we fill our days with interruptions, distractions, and insignificant minutia at the expense of the rocks. Part of this is straight-up procrastination, but another part is the draw of instant gratification. Think about it: How often do you check your phone? Check your calendar? Or look at social media?

How many times a day do brief interruptions in the office take you off course? You may be initiating these distractions yourself by reporting to your team or your colleagues after every client call instead of holding off for a scheduled meeting.

How often do you coach your team with feedback that can wait for another time? Sure, it's best to let people know what they're doing right—or wrong—as soon as possible so they can self-correct their actions and behaviors immediately. But if you're doing it constantly throughout the day, you're not only preventing yourself from getting to those big rocks, you're distracting everyone else too.

Think about all the phone calls and text messages from your partner and kids that you promptly return. Texting the people you love isn't a bad thing, and I'm not insinuating that you should ignore them. But if you weren't going back and forth every hour, you could be using that time to tackle the most important tasks in your day. Then you might be able to leave work early, unwind, and spend some quality time with your family before you sit down to a relaxing dinner. Gee, you might even have something to talk about with them, because you weren't reporting every detail of your day to one another on the phone, by text, and over social media all day. The other payoff would be more time to take care of the rocks, which will have the greatest impact on your life in the long run.

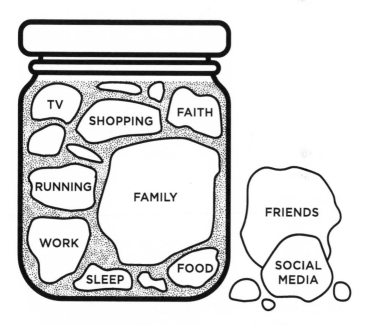

What are your big rocks? What are the major objectives that you have to get to every day? The big rocks might look like they'll never fit in that jar, but they will if you put them in first.

What are your big rocks? What are the major objectives that you have to get to every day? The big rocks might look like they'll never fit in the jar, but they will if you put them in first.

THE EXCEPTION VS. THE RULE

Worry is praying for what you don't want.
—Dr. Kevin Elko

In my office, we have what we call "the exception versus the rule." Planning ahead for future scenarios is part of the job. We're actually *in the business of* preparing people for future situations. But in the day-to-day business of life and work, are we spending too much time on scenarios that have a remote possibility of actually happening?

One of the big rocks in my life is working in the community and running a large wine festival. I'll tell you more about that event later, but for the purposes of this discussion, if someone tells me there's a problem with how we set up the tents or arrange the chairs at the wine festival, I don't immediately respond by changing the arrangement. I want to know why. What is the problem? Well, one person complained. So, one person out of 10,000 did not like the arrangement. How much time should we devote to discussing the matter? It's an exception, and so the answer is "as little time as possible." I'm not saying I don't accept feedback and consider it—but if it's an exception, one person or one possibility—I don't dwell on it. I might put it in the "to be improved" file for next time, but I won't drop everything to spend time on something that rarely happens or has minor consequences.

I get it: we all want to be prepared for what might happen. It's human nature to worry about what might go wrong. But you can't let those thoughts consume you. Being aware of possibilities is extremely important. Focusing a lot of time on them is not. If you're more focused on the exceptions than the rules, it may be time to reprioritize. Instead of the possibilities, look at the *probabilities*. What's probable? We should know the possibilities but plan for what's more likely to happen.

VISUALIZING THE RESULT

We tend to focus on exceptions, but what if we shifted our attention to the result we desire? Visualizing that result, spending time getting to it, and preparing for it is a better use of our time. Instead of thinking through every possible negative before you get to the positive, start with the positive and work your way backwards. If you need to evaluate the exceptions, do it last, after you've visualized the results you want. This approach allows you to stay focused on what you're trying to accomplish.

Visualizing the result helps you identify what you're actually working for so you can commit time to it. Block out time in the day to get there. Just having that time blocked out will make it easier to focus and avoid distractions and interruptions, which can eat up a large part of your day.

If you don't already have a morning routine, create one. Prioritize and execute on the big rocks. Include them in those first few hours of the day—what you need to do to get to the result you visualize.

If you don't think a morning routine makes a difference, here's another exercise you can try. Get a notebook and carry it around with you for a week. Write down everything you do from the time you wake up until around 10 a.m. At the end of the week, see how much time you spent on things that don't matter or aren't getting you toward the result you visualized. You might be surprised by the hours wasted on activities that didn't help you accomplish anything you want to do in your life, and you probably spent time on things that actually moved you in the opposite direction. Journaling like this can be a real eye-opener for some people; it certainly has been for me. An old-school paper journal or a smartphone notes app work well for this.

Start managing your time and focusing on the things you enjoy, are good at, and get you closer to the result you've visualized. At the same time, pay attention to how you feel. Then look at the results. I do this every day, every month, and at the end of the year. Once you start paying attention to yourself and how you spend your time, you might be amazed by what you're capable of accomplishing, and how your day-to-day life can leave you feeling so much more fulfilled.

In an interview with Tim Ferriss, author Jim Collins notes that he tracks his days in a spreadsheet to identify daily, weekly, monthly, and yearly trends. His goal is to spend 50 percent of his time on new, creative, or intellectual activities; 30 percent of his time teaching; and 20 percent doing whatever has to be done. Collins believes that this 50/30/20 breakdown reflects what many of the world's most successful people do.[2] Whether you want to get that granular with your time tracking is up to you; I probably wouldn't put it all in a spreadsheet, but it seems like a good model to follow as a rule of thumb for prioritizing how you spend your time.

YOU ARE THE COMPANY YOU KEEP

Your network of coworkers, clients, and friends often defines who you are and who you can become. In college, I sought out graduates who were working. When I was in my mid-20s, I surrounded myself with 30- and 40-year-olds who had been in the business for awhile. Rather than shying away from people who are more experienced, seek them out and learn from them. Equally important is keeping company with people you respect and whose company you actually enjoy. We all know what "good butterflies" are—that feeling you get in your stomach when something good's about to happen. There are "bad butterflies" too that

2 The Tim Ferriss Show, "#361: Jim Collins—A Rare Interview with a Reclusive Polymath," *Apple Podcasts*, https://podcasts.apple.com/us/podcast/the-tim-ferriss-show/id863897795?i=1000430103992.

make you feel sick or full of dread. If you have colleagues or even clients who give you the bad butterflies every time they call you or you have to be around them, limit your time with those people. This may mean actually breaking up with clients, but if they bother you that much, no amount of money will make them worth your time.

If you've identified your strengths and your blind spots, instead of looking for people who share your weaknesses, look for people who can fill in those blind spots for you with their own knowledge. You can find mentors among your colleagues and at networking events, and you can hire professional coaches to help elevate your game. Business coach Steve Moeller wrote the book *Effort-Less Marketing for Financial Advisors*, which I read more than a decade ago. At the time, I felt like that book was written just for me, but I was working for someone else and couldn't implement a lot of Steve's teachings. I hung onto the book, and as soon as I was in a position to start putting the lessons to work, I actually called Steve. It turned out that he had a coaching platform, and I signed up. Working with him was so easy. He understood where I wanted to go and helped me build the business. I'd been coaching other advisors, and now having my own coach was an instrumental transition. I started executing on a whole new level. Steve made me question what I had been taught and got me to open my mind to a lot of new ideas. We were able to build things together that helped change the trajectory of my practice.

I've also taken Matt Oeschli's six-month training program to get a better understanding of what my team of advisors' experiences were like from their points of view. Over the years, I've always reached out to others whenever I feel I need it. Coaches, professional networks, and formal training are all ways to improve your skills while putting you in the company of people you actually want to keep.

Again, when you're seeking out people to spend time with, consider your personality traits and how other people can complement what you have to offer. I'm an idea person, so if I surround myself with people who help execute, I'm successful. If I surround myself with a bunch of idea people, we'll have amazing conversations, but no one will write down any of our ideas, much less actually execute them.

My model for business is the Beatles. They were four guys who kept each other's negative tendencies in check. They balanced each other and the total was greater than the sum parts. And that's how I see business. Great things in business are never done by one person, they are done by a team of people.
—Steve Jobs

LEAVE WORK ON THE TABLE

Finding balance demands that you sometimes leave work on the table. Don't worry—it will be there when you get back. There will always be more to do, and you will never catch up, so recognize that fact and accept it. You can be very productive by managing your time, but even if you do everything on your list, there will be a whole new list in the morning. This is where having a journal or planner can help. I've had days when I left the office with a pile of work on my desk thinking, *Wow, it seems like I got nothing done!* But I look at my planner and realize I got a lot done—just not everything. If you have an unexpected call or meeting in the day, add that to your planner. Take credit for it. Then when you look back at your calendar, task list, planner, or however you track your time, you won't feel so bad about leaving a few things undone. If you've prioritized, those last few tasks aren't going to make or break your business anyway.

WHAT ARE YOU WORKING FOR?

During the financial crisis in 2008, I saw the financial challenges as an opportunity to transform our company. We were all going to struggle for a while, so what better time to get a better handle on how to make the business more efficient and purpose driven. I had just started working with Steve Moeller, and he gave me a worksheet to fill out that asked the questions, *What am I working for? What are my goals? What is my five-year vision?*

I filled it out: what I wanted to do with my time, what I wanted to have, and what I wanted my life to look like. I wanted a bigger house for my family, and a pool big enough that I could invite all the relatives over to swim in it. I wanted to coach my kids in sports. I wanted a lot of things—mostly related to family, travel, and community—and writing them all down put my work into perspective.

> A Harvard Business Study found that the 3 percent of MBA graduates who had their goals written down ended up earning ten times as much as the other 97 percent put together, just ten years after graduation.[3]

I put the list away, but a few years later I happened to find it, and guess what? Everything I had written had come true. I don't know if writing down these goals and vision drove me to make them happen, but the exercise made me think honestly about what I really wanted beyond the day-to-day and week-to-week objectives in life. I had to think bigger and decide what was really worth working toward.

Since I had accomplished those goals, I recalibrated, thinking about what I was working for next; then I made a habit of updating the worksheet regularly. Some years I was working for more time for travel, or more things for me or my family. Some years I saw that other people needed my help, like a relative, so I was working for them. Other times, my community involvement required more time and attention, so I had to work more for that.

Just being conscious of why you do what you do, and revisiting those reasons, can put purpose in your life. You're

---

3   Sid Savara, "Why 3% of Harvard MBAs Make Ten Times as Much as the Other 97% Combined," *Sid Savara*, https://sidsavara.com/why-3-of-harvard-mbas-make-ten -times-as-much-as-the-other-97-combined/.

not bringing home a paycheck just to pay the bills; you are devoting time to a cause that matters to you. Lots of songs reference investing in love is really investing in life. Truer words were never spoken. The way I see it, *Time=Love* and *Love=Time*, yet often we put time into loving the wrong things. Just as I had discovered on that trip to Bourbon Country, the relationships that I put time into were precious, and working to make them stronger with my time and my love gave my life purpose and paid off with everything that mattered most to me.

We all expect to get a return on our investments, but we first have to make that investment. We might be investing our money, our time, or our love, but we have to work for something to get something.

HOW DO YOU SPEND YOUR TIME?

We all make assumptions about how we spend our days. Tracking your time will tell you the truth about how you spend it. David Bach's *The Latte Factor: Why You Don't Have to Be Rich to Live Rich* describes how people fritter away cash on things like pricey cups of coffee without considering how much all those four-dollar lattes add up to over time. When you do a time inventory, you'll likely discover a similar latte factor, where you're wasting time on unnecessary tasks out of habit.

In an eight-hour workday, you might spend an hour on social media, an hour chitchatting with colleagues, and another hour on the phone, email, or text, having conversations about all kinds of things that have nothing to do with your priorities. Do you have a stack of great books on your desk or nightstand that you keep meaning to get to but never have time? Imagine if you shifted all that time on Facebook to reading those books, or to writing a blog on LinkedIn that's useful to your clients or colleagues.

You might be using distractions as a break from work. One very popular distraction (I know, because I've done it!) is managing your inbox, or worse, pretending to manage your inbox without actually dealing with the emails. You move them from one folder to another, telling yourself it's necessary work. Instead, take a cue from Ari Meisel: delete, do, or defer.[4] Scrolling through emails and moving them around is a delay tactic that accomplishes absolutely nothing. Well, your priorities aren't getting any attention while you're pretending to organize your inbox. That doesn't mean you shouldn't do it—just be honest with yourself about it. And if you need a break and want to scroll, *try* to do it productively. Don't pretend that giving in to distractions is anything other than an escape or a form of procrastination, which it is. So if your time has so little value, or you have so much extra time, that you can afford to blow it on a Distraction Grande, then go for it. But if you value your time, spend it where it counts. And if you really need a break, take a break—a real break. Do something you truly enjoy doing.

Be honest about how you spend your time, and take steps to better manage it. By letting go of distractions like

---

4   Ari Meisel, The Art of Doing Less: One Entrepreneur's Formula for a Beautiful Life (Austin: Lioncrest, 2016).

social media that dictate your schedule, you will actually have more time and more freedom to create the rich life you want.

If you want to really know how you're spending your time, start tracking it. Then do an audit. Apps like RescueTime automatically track your computer and mobile device time by application and website so you can see how much time you spend on different activities. You can do this manually with Clockify or Toggl, or just write it down in a notebook or day planner. Your iPhone will track the amount of time you spend on social media. You might be surprised by how much time you spend on pebbles and sand, and begin to understand why you never have enough time for the big rocks.

LOVE YOURSELF ENOUGH TO CHANGE

We all believe that we love ourselves, but our behavior often tells a different tale. We eat food that we know isn't good for us, waste our limited time on stuff that doesn't matter, and spend money frivolously. We sabotage our lives every day with bad habits. Then we use excuses to justify it:

"I would have eaten a salad for lunch, but the burger joint was on my way back from that appointment."

"I would have bought just one burger, but it was 2-4-1 Tuesday so I got two of everything, and now I won't have to spend so much on dinner."

"I would have gone to the gym after work, but I was feeling kind of sluggish from that big lunch."

I believe that you do love yourself enough to change, but some of us need help. In *The Power of Habit*[5], Charles Duhigg discusses how to break a habit. He defines "habit" in three stages: cue, routine, and reward. The cue triggers the habit; for example, going into the kitchen in the morning might be your cue to make coffee. The routine is the actual behavior that defines the habit—in this example, drinking the coffee. Finally, the reward is the smell and taste of the coffee. It's the payoff you get for maintaining that habit. Your brain "spikes" twice during these stages: at the cue stage and again at the reward stage, which reinforces the habit. Repeating the habit strengthens it, making it harder to break. This is good news if you're trying to create a good habit, but not so good when you've developed a bad habit that you want to break. Duhigg recommends focusing on the cue stage to break a habit.

Say you're a nail-biter. Rather than trying to simply stop biting your fingernails, figure out what causes you to bite your nails. Maybe you rub your fingers together and find a rough spot or a hangnail, and that's what causes you to put your fingers in your mouth and chew those nails. What triggers you to rub your fingers together? Is it stress? The next time you chew a nail, think about what created that stress. That is your trigger, your cue, and what you need to correct in order to stop biting your fingernails.

This takes self-awareness, and so you have to love yourself enough to become self-aware. What are you doing to

---

5   Charles Duhigg, *The Power of Habit: Why We Do What We Do in Life and Business* (New York: Random House, 2012).

sabotage your time, your life? We wouldn't sabotage other people's lives this way, yet we treat ourselves this way all the time.

WHAT FREEDOM MEANS TO YOU

Freedom means different things to different people. For some, freedom is having a more balanced life, with fewer hours spent at work and more time with family. For others, freedom is an easier, less stressful workday, which might come with a better schedule and discipline. Still others define freedom as finding the 80/20 balance where they're spending 80 percent of their time with their favorite people or doing the top 20 percent of the activities they enjoy most.

Living a rich life begins with defining what freedom means to you. I can give you many ideas about what that means, but really, you need to evaluate your own life, thoughts, and feelings, and decide for yourself what freedom means to you.

As you're considering your next stage and your exit strategy, think about where you are emotionally. Are you prepared to move on? Are you ready to explore new partnerships, new endeavors, a new niche? We'll talk about the logistics of your next stage, but first, let's talk about where you are in your own head. This is really no different than the hundreds of conversations you've had with clients. How many times has someone walked into your office with this story?

"I've been working for forty-eight years. I get up at four-thirty every day and come home at seven. On the weekends,

I play golf and putter around the house. I want to retire in six months."

You say, "That's terrific. And what are you going to do then?"

Nine times out of ten, the response is, "I have no idea."

They really don't know, because they haven't even "gone there" in their mind yet. They haven't thought through what not getting up at 4:30 every day will be like, or how they are going to fill their days until 7 o'clock.

We as advisors have to have this same conversation with ourselves before we can move on.

It's not as bad as it sounds, especially if you don't like playing golf or doing chores. You could be thinking about a second career. You might want to merge with another business and work fewer hours, so you can have four-day weekends. Whatever your next stage is, think about what it will look like. Without a plan, you don't know. So think about what you want it to look like. What could you be doing in that next stage that would make you feel the happiest, the most fulfilled?

ALL YOU NEED IS LOVE

I lost two of my grandparents last year, and had the honor of delivering their eulogies. I didn't begin by telling everyone in the room about my grandparents' work successes. No one wanted to know about their careers or what they owned. They wanted to hear all the really good stuff about my grandparents, and that's what I talked about.

People who cared about my grandparents wanted to know only one thing: What did my grandparents love? Relatives wanted to remember these people for the friendships they nurtured, children they raised, charities they supported, and stories they told. Whatever made my grandparents smile was what everyone wanted to know about. That's what we remember about people: where they put their love.

It's the same for anyone. When a financial advisor passes away, don't expect to hear about how many phone calls they made or reports they created. You might hear that they loved their work. But mostly what you will hear is where the person put their love.

We don't always put our love where it belongs. Just like we have to recalibrate what we're working for, we need to recalibrate where we're putting our love, too. If we get that right, everything else falls into place.

As you move through the phases of your career, revisit where you're putting your love. When you first start out, be aware of who you're taking on as clients and decide whether these are the kind of people you can love or not. Is this the kind of work you can love? Be honest with yourself. You may need to make a change. As you move forward in your business, look to add more people and more work that you will be happy to give your love to.

Beyond work, find love in other parts of your life. If you don't, you will never be able to step away from the work. Some people work for decades, and the thought of separating from their business terrifies them, because they have nothing and no one they love enough to replace the work. This is more common than you think. I've worked with advisors who retired, yet continued to show up at the office because they had nowhere else to go. There was no love beyond their job.

CHAPTER THREE QUESTIONS

1. What are your rocks, pebbles, and sand? How much time do you spend on them each day, week, and month?

2. Are you spending time on creative activities, or simple tasks?

3. What does your 50/30/20 look like? Can you visualize the results if you followed that plan?

4. Do you have a coach or a mentor that challenges you to be a better version of yourself? Are you accountable to anyone when it comes to your life?

5. Where are you investing your love?

6. What does freedom mean to you?

PART I ACTION PLAN

1. Audit your time using an application or manually. Do this for one month. Now think about how much time you should be spending on each activity or task to achieve Financial Freedom. Write those numbers down and then try to achieve them.

2. Make a list of your top ten relationships—the people who you would miss the most if you were never to see them again. Write down their names, then write down the last personal gesture or favor you did for them. Do they know that you appreciate their friendship?

3. Find a journal or a planner that you like and write down what you have to do each day, and what you accomplish every day. Make a point to skim the list every day and recognize all the work you've done. If you have to leave a few things on your desk until tomorrow so you can spend some time with your friends or family after work, don't beat yourself up— that work will be waiting for you in the morning.

PART II

Living Your Legacy

No one has ever become poor by giving.
—Anne Frank

As advisors, we impact people every day.

I've heard stories of advisors changing people's lives. For example, an advisor told me about one of his clients who was planning a trip. The client told him, "My wife and I have never been out West. She's never been farther than Tennessee, and I've never been west of Missouri." But because of this advisor's connection to the client, their process of serving them, as well as helping them connect all the dots, they were able to chart a plan that allowed them to see the entire country.

This is the kind of daily impact we have on people's lives, and it's what contributes to our legacy. There are grander impacts, too, and we'll get to those in the following chapters. But don't overlook, or take for granted, these smaller impacts. To you, they are part of your everyday life as an advisor, but they have a huge impact on the lives of those you serve.

I attended a wake for a client and was standing in line along with about a hundred other people to pay my condolences to the man's wife. He hadn't included her in any of his financial decisions and all the accounts were in his name, so I had never met the woman. When I introduced myself, she confessed that she didn't know anything about the family's finances and didn't even know whether she could pay the mortgage that month. This was heartbreaking: here we were celebrating her deceased husband's life, and she was crying her eyes out, worried about finances. That Monday I was at her house, helping her locate life insurance policies and explaining her husband's accounts to her so she could pay her bills.

I had another client for many years until he was in hospice care. He checked himself out of the hospice for a few days and came to see my team. He thanked each one of us and told us that we had played an important part in his life and legacy. This man's primary legacy goal was to take care of his family. In our office that day, he had a stack of papers—all the documents he was leaving to his wife. He plucked the top page from the stack and showed it to me. My name was written at the top. "Do you see this?" he asked. "It's what I'm giving my wife. Everything she needs to know and everyone she needs to call is in here." He shook my hand and left, and I was in tears. To have that man's trust meant everything to me. It also reminded me why I take the responsibility as seriously as I do caring for my own family.

CHAPTER 4

Your Legacy Today

We make a living by what we get.
We make a life by what we give.
—Winston S. Churchill

I'm a genuinely positive person who doesn't spend time focusing on the negatives in life. But even I have an occasional bad day when everything seems to go wrong.

That's what happened one Tuesday. I loaded the kids into the SUV to drive them to school, and the Tahoe's battery was dead. I planned to jumpstart it, but the vehicle was pulled so far into the garage that I couldn't get the cables to it from my work truck. Running late, we all got in the truck, and I dropped the kids off at the bus stop and kept driving all the way to Norfolk, where I had a meeting. I missed the exit completely, had to backtrack, couldn't find a parking spot, and finally showed up fifteen minutes late. I felt awful making my appointment wait, and I spent extra time with them to make up for it.

After the meeting, a friend met me back at the house with a portable battery charger. We got the Tahoe running, then I drove all over town trying (unsuccessfully) to get a new battery at two different automotive shops, finally ending up at the dealership. Instead of having lunch like I usually do that time of day, I spent what felt like all day getting a new battery.

Sitting there in the dealership's waiting room, I got a call from the office. There was a fire that needed putting out, and even though my people could take care of it, I felt like I needed to get back quickly. The problem wasn't only frustrating; it could cost us a lot of money, so I skipped lunch and rushed back to the office. Everything was fine, but by then it was 3 o'clock in the afternoon, and I felt like most of the day had been a total waste. Feeling stressed out, tired, hungry, and defeated, I laid my head on my desk and wondered what else could go wrong. I remember thinking to myself, *Scott, you don't have bad days. But if you did, this is exactly what a bad day would look like.*

That's when my phone buzzed. It was a text from Leah, one of the directors at the local Boys and Girls Club, where I'm on the board. She rarely asks me for anything, but she knows that when she does, I always respond.

Years ago, during a Christmas toy drive, the club had collected very few toys for all the kids. Leah had asked for my advice, and I told her to tell me about the twelve kids who needed help the most: *who were they, and what was their family situation?* If we were going to get people to care, we had to make it personal. We had to put faces on the toy drive so people who contributed would understand that they weren't just helping fill a box; they were making a difference in the lives of real people. I had taken the information Leah sent me and presented it to my Rotary Club and—to make a long story short—we now deliver toys to *all* the kids in need in our Boys and Girls Club every year, plus children who are outside the club, and we bring their families a holiday dinner on Christmas Eve. The whole drive kind of exploded, to where we end up with a truckload of toys every year, and Leah never has to worry about coming up short for these kids.

Anyway, here I was, on a day that was really testing my positive attitude. I lifted my head from my desk to read the text. It wasn't anywhere near the holidays, so I had no idea why Leah would be contacting me. The way my day was going so far, what else could possibly go wrong?

Hey Scott, I read, *one of my families is going to be homeless tonight and we're short $380. Do you think it would be okay to reach out to the board, or do you know anybody that I can lean on?*

I texted her back: *Tell me about the family.*

Every day, we make choices that define our legacies by the deeds we do, the choices we make, and how we live our lives. We live our legacies day in and day out, in the impacts we make and relationships we create. Your legacy isn't what you create at the end of your lifetime; it's what you did yesterday, and what you'll do today and tomorrow. Did you listen to someone today? Did you help a person in any capacity? Our legacies are determined by the choices we make every day and the impacts those choices make on people and causes we believe in.

When you're stepping down from your practice or separating from your business, you are building on your legacy. If you make your exit all about the business, you're not going to be happy with the legacy you leave behind. But if you leave your employees and your clients in a good place, you will have a legacy to be proud of. Think of your next stage in life as a new chapter. You're eager to embrace this new world. You see it as an opportunity to express your gratitude for all the years you enjoyed the company of those people, while looking forward to your family who has supported you at home.

But before you even get to that stage, be thinking about the legacy you're building every day. When I asked Leah to tell me about the family, I was inviting these people into my life. With the day I was having, I didn't need more problems. I didn't need more to do either. But instead of seeing it that way, I saw the text message as an opportunity for me to make a positive impact that day. I could sit at my desk and stew about my bad day, or I could accept this invitation to make a positive impact in another person's life.

My cell buzzed again. Leah: *Single mom, Scott, and she's got four kids. They're in an efficiency in a hotel and Mom's paycheck cycle is off by one week, so she won't get paid until Thursday. The rent's due today and they're kicking the family out if it's not paid by the end of the day. Oh, and we're supposed to get rain tonight.*

I wanted to know more. *Tell me about the mom's job. What does she do?*

Leah: *Mom's a manager at Taco Bell and she works double shifts almost every day.* A pause, then, *Scott, she deserves our help. I've $80 together from my family and friends. We need $300 more. How do you think I should proceed with our board?*

I texted, *What's your Venmo?* referring to her mobile payment number. She texted me back, and I sent her the $300.

Have you ever asked a higher power, or asked yourself, to find the strength to get through something? Maybe you were struggling financially, or your kid was being bullied, or you had a big presentation and didn't feel 100 percent confident in yourself. *Please, just let me get through this.*

When you're in a situation like that, don't ask for help. Look for what you can do to help someone else. In the moment I decided to send Leah that money, I wasn't thinking about how I could personally benefit. The woman and her kids wouldn't know the money came from me, so there would be no thank you; I wouldn't even have the pleasure of seeing the look on her face when Leah handed her the cash. That didn't matter. The payoff, for me, was worth much more than a few hundred bucks.

For one, I immediately felt better. In minutes, I went from head on the desk, wondering how much worse my day would get, to sitting up, shoulders back, and grinning from ear to ear. From there, my whole day changed. My mindset shifted and I was energized, like a weight had been lifted off my shoulders.

Then my cell rang. It was Leah, and she was crying. "Scott," she said, "You have no idea what this means. You did not have to do that, and I can't thank you enough."

She went to see the woman right after our call, paid the rent, and the family still lives in that same hotel with her kids. More importantly, they didn't have their lives disrupted and didn't have to be homeless for a week, carrying their belongings around with them, wondering where they would sleep and how they would eat.

My bad day turned out to be a wonderful day that I'll never forget, because I made an impact on the lives of six people—Leah, the mom, and those four kids. Those are the incremental deeds that I see as my legacy that I live every single day.

Leah must have told someone about it, because at the next Boys and Girls Club board meeting, the area CEO and president stood in front of about forty members and told that story. He added, "Listen, we tend to think we're just here to make big decisions. But don't forget about the little decisions you can make every day that affect just one person or one family. Those count, too."

Living your legacy is about making an impact beyond what you do in your day-to-day work. Of course, we all want to make a positive impact on the people we serve in our practices. We also want purpose in our day. A life without purpose feels empty. Finding a purpose that serves others changes how you approach your work, your life, the world, and the people in it.

USE YOUR PLATFORM

As financial advisors, we have a platform that not everyone else has. What we do with it is up to us—it's how we live our legacy. Visit a local charity and you'll see the big donors are inevitably businesses, and advisory practices are often at or near the top of the list. Those advisors understand the fulfillment that comes with purpose and making an impact in their communities. They've discovered their platforms and are leveraging them to live their legacies every day.

As an advisor, you may not want to accept that platform. But think of other people in similar situations, such as athletes. Like you, they are in a position to affect great change, and many use that platform generously. When Hurricane Harvey hit Houston in 2017, an estimated 27 trillion gallons of rain fell over Texas and parts of Louisiana over a span of six days. It was estimated the total recovery could require upwards of $200 billion. J. J. Watt, a defensive player for the Houston Texans, initially set out to raise $200,000 to assist those affected in southeast Texas but raised more than $37 million. NBA superstar LeBron James of the LA Lakers built schools for at-risk third and fourth graders last year. His foundation plans to expand the schools to first through eighth grade by 2022. James has promised these children free tuition to the University of Akron. Others prefer to just be seen as a basketball player or football player, not as a role model or leader among their fans. Yes, they were born gifted and worked hard to get where they are. But each of them also had an opportunity, and they acted on it. Unfortunately, not every talented kid gets an opportunity to be a pro, no matter how hard they work.

It's the same for successful advisors. You may not have fans per se, but you also have talents and worked hard to get where you are. Like an athlete, despite all the challenges you've been through, the circumstances were also somehow in your favor to get where you are. Because of your financial success, people look to you and they notice how you move through the world. Using that platform, whether you're donating money or helping someone out another way, sends a message that you are aware of your position and you don't take it for granted.

Be open to those opportunities to use your platform. You'll miss most of them. I still do. I have days when there is so much going on that I'm not open to what else is happening around me. I'm not always focused on how I can make a positive impact. But if I can identify just one out of every dozen, I'm doing more than if I shut myself off to them entirely.

I've gotten in the habit of keeping a hundred-dollar bill in my wallet. I almost always pay with a card, but that money is for special, unexpected occasions. Like the time I was in the airport in Atlanta, waiting at a restaurant bar to order a salad and a glass of wine. The staff was in chaos, two of them were actually shouting at each other, and no one was getting served. The bartender didn't get the water I ordered, and they were out of every type of wine I liked. But I could see the pained look on her face, and I didn't want to add to all the pressure. So I made a deal with her: We're going to smile and make it better for one another, because we both want more out of this day. Let's not let it ruin our day. She agreed and got me the salad and some wine. Then she said, "I've been here since 2 a.m., and I wasn't supposed to work two back-to-back shifts. I'm just exhausted, so I'm sorry for everything."

I told her I understood, and that I and everyone else at the bar were going to do what we could to make the rest of her shift enjoyable. She smiled and other people joined in, telling her she was doing a great job. The whole vibe changed from one of high stress to relaxed laughter. The bill came to twenty-two bucks, and I left the hundred-dollar bill. "Keep the change," I said. The woman thanked me with tears in her eyes. I have no idea what was going on at that place, but instead of focusing on how it affected my day, I looked at what was happening to someone else. I could have walked out and gone to a different restaurant. That bartender was stuck there, though, and leaving would mean passing up an opportunity to do something nice for one person. After a very long day and several flights, I didn't go home that night grumbling about the lousy service at the airport bar. I arrived with a smile on my face, feeling like a million bucks.

I've had other opportunities fall in my lap. I don't go around handing out hundreds of dollars every month, but when the situation warrants it, I know that helping another person has as much of an impact on my life as theirs.

I've helped people who were down on their luck, too, and even though it's easier than ever to research people on the internet these days to see if their story is true, I tend not to worry about it so much. An Uber driver I met, for example, was having a tough time. He also worked as an assistant pastor, but his life had been derailed. His wife had kicked him out of the house and taken up with another man, and this guy was living in an apartment and trying to get his life together, driving part-time to pay the bills. I did leave the man a very large tip, and I felt good doing it. Was his story real? I don't know. I believed him. The important thing here is what it did for me.

Dr. Kevin Elko tells a story of an international pro golfer who won $100,000, and as he was leaving the course, a woman came up to him crying. She said her daughter was dying of cancer and they couldn't afford surgery. The golfer signed over the oversized fake check to her and instructed the tournament director to give the woman his winnings. Soon after this happened, the man was told that he had been scammed. The woman had lied to him and, in fact, didn't even have a daughter. But she had his $100,000. The golfer's response wasn't what you'd expect.

"Wait a second, let me get this straight," he said. "There's no sick child dying of cancer? That's the best news I've heard all day."

I don't share these stories to show I'm a good guy but to just use some real-life examples that have reminded me to pay attention to the things around me. Many times I've found that I missed chances to make a difference. Later in life, I realized those opportunities were right in front of me.

This isn't only about money, but if you're a successful advisor, you might have some to spare. So why not look for ways to use what you have to make a difference for others? Focusing only on yourself will leave you unfulfilled, while serving other people and a higher purpose is life changing.

ARE YOUR NETWORKS WIDE AND DEEP?

Advisors are in a unique position to see how our work affects people every day. Think about the conversations you have with your clients. They share the details of one of the most intimate, and often most taboo, subjects that rule their lives: their finances. Outside of the financial world, people typically don't talk about money. They don't tell their friends how much money they make or how much debt they have. Yet these same people share all the details of their financial situation with their advisor.

In our world, creating a rich life can often be misguided. When you deal with money all the time, you become numb to all the emotions attached to it. It's nothing for me to ask another advisor what they make in a year, but can you imagine asking your neighbor that question? I can't even get a straight answer out of my own mother, and I manage her finances. Talking about money is uncomfortable for most people. There's a reason so many marriages end in divorce, and why so many divorces are caused by finances. Most people don't talk about it because it's such a sensitive topic, and those of us who do have forgotten how sensitive it is.

For advisors, it's not always such an emotional discussion—money is a big part of what we do and who we are. It's our job to change the conversation for our clients, to make it easier for them to talk about money. We need to make money a less taboo subject for everyone, and we can start by viewing our clients and their money concerns with a little more heart. Beyond all the "wide" relationships we have with clients, we need to dig deep and create some depth, too. We create that depth by discovering what's different about them, what's most important to them, and what single thing we could do for them that would be life changing.

You help your clients plan for the best in life and prepare for the worst. The decisions they make, under your guidance, affect their lives in many ways, including their ability to own a home, buy a car, go on vacation, send their kids to college, and retire knowing that they will be taken care of financially. Ultimately, they want to know that the people they care about will be taken care of financially after they pass on. Who else in the professional world is trusted with so many important decisions in a person's life?

I can't emphasize this enough. Finances are very personal. People who share the same financial values have that connection in common. This might be why our financial conversations often become relationship conversations: how the decisions our clients make affect their closest relationships, for better or for worse. In these conversations, people show you who they are financially. And quite honestly, they're *naked*. When a person shares the details of all their financial successes and failures, they're often embarrassed by their missteps. It's not always a proud feeling, telling someone the whole truth about your money. It's very personal—like standing in front of a mirror and exposing yourself for who you truly are, instead of the person you typically show the world.

Advisors must be respectful of that vulnerability. It's where the real human connection occurs. It's why we celebrate our clients' highpoints in life, and why we grieve with them during the lows. It's why we go to their weddings and their funerals, and why we cry at both.

By the nature of our day-to-day work, advisors have the gift of insight. We already know what it feels like to make a difference in the lives of others. We've enjoyed the rewards of making an impact, having a purpose, and building on our legacy every day with every contact. It's natural for us to want to do more of that.

THREE THINGS

Several years ago, I attended a John Maxwell leadership conference with a good friend, Dexter. The lead speaker was Dr. Rohm, who's a leading behavioral psychiatrist and teacher on the model of human behaviors and personality. Somehow Dexter got himself invited to the doctor's penthouse at the Orlando World Conference Center. He texted me that evening and asked me to come up. I went and ended up in a room with a sports agent, two Olympians—a gymnast and a wrestler—a professional football player, two people from the John Maxwell leadership team, along with Dr. Rohm and my friend Dexter.

Dr. Rohm had hired Zig Ziglar to mentor him when he first got into business, and he told us about one of his first conversations with the man. He said they were sitting at a kitchen table, and he said to Ziglar, "I've always been chasing money. I can't seem to catch it. Every time I turn around, payroll's due and I feel like I'm barely going to make it, or I feel like I'm just tight all the time, and no matter how good

I get in business, I'm behind. I feel like I can't catch it."

Zig said to him, "The more you chase money, the less chance you have at ever catching it. In fact, you'll never catch it if you're chasing it." He continued, "I've learned there are only three things that you need to do, and if you do these three things, the money will be chasing you:

"Number one is you need to help people."

Easy enough to agree with that; probably all people do, right? Deep down, when you help someone else, you feel good. If your business revolves around helping other people, you have a great start. Financial advisors' careers literally revolve around helping people, so we have that one in the bag, and we get it. We know how good it feels to help people.

Rohm continued with his story about Zig Ziglar:

"Number two is turning a profit," Zig told him. "I can't tell you how many people I meet who want to help people, but they don't want to turn a profit. They actually feel like turning a profit and helping people conflict."

I agree with Zig on that point, and I think a lot of the "I'm making money" guilt some advisors feel often comes from an early life of poverty or a place where one lacks self-worth. If you can turn a profit by helping people, you have number one and number two down; but if you're helping people and not making any money, you won't be in business very long. An advisor who helps people for free all the time won't be able to support themselves or their family, and they won't have anything to give back to their community.

Dr. Rohm continued with his Zig story.

"Number three," Zig said, "is that you've got to serve something bigger than yourself. If you're doing all of this for yourself, you will be empty." Zig told him that he serves God. "Serving God gives me a purpose that's much bigger than myself every day."

Dr. Rohm said that what Zig told him changed how he approached money. He stopped chasing it and started focusing on helping people while turning a profit and serving God, or at least something bigger than himself.

A week later, he was in a meeting with a business that was hiring him to do personality tests and other assessments. After the meeting, he wound up in an elevator with a man he'd never met. The man asked him what kind of work he did, and after a short conversation, he asked Dr. Rohm if they could meet in his offices. He wanted Rohm to help him out at his company.

The man in the elevator, it turned out, was the founder and owner of a very large company. Within a week, the doctor was the keynote speaker at a presentation for the Canadian branch of the business, speaking to thousands of representatives.

Rohm worked with these people, teaching them how to better communicate, not by learning about themselves, but by listening to other people and seeking to understand what they need. Personality assessments that provide insight about a person are useful, but this was different. His approach was about acknowledging people's individuality and our need to tailor our communication—how we transmit and receive it—to better connect.

Dr. Rohm told us, "I called Zig and told him what I had changed, and what had happened. He wasn't surprised. Ultimately, I had made a conscious effort to do the three things that he had told me to do."

A HIGHER PURPOSE

That story gave me a sense of validation for everything I had been doing, and I had an epiphany: I was on the right path, and rather than question it, I needed to go all in.

For starters, I went back to church. I hadn't been going regularly for a while, but for the next three months, I attended morning mass Monday through Friday. I needed peace, and I needed to think. Church was where I could do that, and it was during those hours that I realized Zig was right, Dr. Rohm was right. Because anytime I served something bigger than myself, I won, and the people around me won too. That was when I made the decision to follow the same path with my own independent financial practice.

I was involved in local charities and in my community at the time but had never appreciated the impact I could have and the difference I could make if I channeled my efforts with this new intent of serving a higher purpose.

I attended a national conference where the founder of Zappos, Tony Hsieh, was speaking. I expected to hear him talk about business, but Tony talked about something else: finding his purpose. He told us how he had moved his business to a rough section of Las Vegas, and how that had led to him making an impact on the community. It showed him that his real purpose wasn't just running a business, it was improving people's lives. Tony had invested $50 to $100 million in small businesses, providing grants to people and letting them run their companies out of offices on the bottom floor of Zappos' headquarters.

Zappos had bought an old municipal building. Instead of gating the place off from the community like so many large corporations do, he opened it up and made it part of the community. He runs his business that way, too, with a focus on the community and how his business impacts the people in it.

Tony offered to send anyone a copy of the presentation, and the words were no sooner out of his mouth when I shot him an email: "Listen, this is everything that I believe in. I'd love a copy of your presentation." I forwarded it to a few city leaders who were also business owners, to show them what I wanted to do and what I thought maybe they should be doing too.

Tony didn't wait to retire to make a difference in his community. He started living his legacy years ago, and he tied it to his business.

BUILDING COMMUNITY FIRST
Business owners often set out to build their business first, and then focus on building their community. I see it differently. If you start by looking at what you can do for your community and work to build it up, your community will rise and lift your business with it. The key is to direct your

focus on what works for you and your business, and what means something to you. Otherwise, you might find yourself on numerous boards or involved in a lot of charitable events that are worthwhile but take up so much of your time and energy that you won't be able to make any kind of real impact in any one pursuit.

Some people wait until they've been in business for decades before they take an interest in bettering their community. I can't tell you how many times I've heard from a new board member introducing himself or herself, "I've been in business for thirty years and decided it's time to start giving back." Imagine what they could have accomplished in their communities and with their business if they had started giving back thirty years earlier!

If you feel like you can't give back right now because of family obligations, fair enough. We all work a lot, and having time with family is incredibly important. But that doesn't mean you can't find some time once a month to do something, and maybe even involve your families. Show them what you do and show them the impact you make. Be that role model, so when they grow up and start their own businesses, you won't have to explain why having a purpose bigger than themselves is important. They can start doing it right away instead of waiting thirty years into their careers.

Think big, not just in business, but in what you can do for others. It doesn't have to be writing a check. In fact, donating your time can have a great impact on others and also on the person who volunteers their time. In our industry, advisors often sponsor causes financially, but they avoid giving their time. Donating money to a good cause counts for a lot—without donations, many worthwhile projects wouldn't survive. However, the return on investment of donating your time is even greater because of how it changes you, the donor. On the most basic level, compare writing a check to the American Red Cross with actually taking the time to donate blood. Now compare that with volunteering one day a year to assist with the blood drive. Which of these three gestures has the greatest human ROI? Which experience is most likely to change who you are and how you view the world?

Again, I'm not trying to take anything away from financial donations. Donor money builds hospitals and university medical campuses. It pays for cancer centers. My own annual charitable event relies on checks from a lot of people, and I'm very, very thankful to them. But aside from the finances, finding a way to donate some time every month, or at least once a year, will change you. You may find out that you love it so much that it will become part of your legacy.

You might also find a way to generate more money for your cause by giving your time. You might be able to donate $1,000 to a charity, but what if you could dedicate your passion and skills toward an event that raises millions?

Advisors spend all day helping people, and we can easily burn out. The impact we have isn't always obvious. Even when we're making a great paycheck, we might feel like we're not making the kind of impact we'd like to in the world. Or we might feel like our business is our ministry and we're already helping so many people, why should we have to do more?

I'm not diminishing that work at all, just asking you to think bigger. When you begin to take steps away from your business and to the next stage, having that time in the community will give you a stepping-stone to continue building your legacy.

BE THE PROPHET, NOT THE GOD

If everything in your business is about you being in control, and if you believe you're the only person who can answer questions, make decisions, and put out fires, then you've pretty much made yourself the god of your business. As long as the business revolves only around you, you are always the god. You might feel important, but taking on that role decreases the value of your business. What you do isn't repeatable or scalable. Your business can't survive without you, so it's more or a less a hobby. Without you, the business dies.

It becomes more difficult to sell a business that you control as if you're a god. However, it's easier to sell a business that you lead more like a prophet. The defining factor here is a prophet works through others and can replicate the messaging for mass distribution, a god is the end-all, the only one. This means developing your team and processes so the business can run with you or without you.

Business leaders like to develop themselves, but if they're not developing the people around them, they're not really leading—they're just telling people what to do. Less telling and more teaching are key to becoming a prophet who empowers your people and enriches your business. It also allows you to have time for other things. If you can't take a few days off because the business can't support your absence, that's nothing to be proud of. *You need a break!*

I've known advisors who can't separate for one week. They casually speak about their importance, a "humble brag," but being indispensable is not something I'd brag about. It means that you're essentially trapped. Operating that way will never get you to Freedom Street.

I did this for a long time, by the way. I'd take on every administrative task, telling myself, "If I don't do it myself, it won't be done right." But if your staff can't handle anything without you there, think about who hired and trained them. Look at who they look to for guidance. You're the role model, and it's on you to bring your people up so they can take on whatever is required of them.

I'm not diminishing the impact an advisor makes within their practice. If you're making an impact every day, be proud of that. But don't think that's all you can do. You can serve clients one by one, or you can train your advisors and the rest of your staff to serve them too. Adopt a growth mindset. As John C. Maxwell said, "Leadership is influence, nothing more, nothing less."[6] Leadership *is* influence, and if your influence grows, so does your impact.

One day you'll wake up and decide that the day has

---

6   John C. Maxwell, The 21 Irrefutable Laws of Leadership: Follow Them and People Will Follow You, 10th ed., (Nashville: Thomas Nelson, 2007).

come for you to exit the business by selling it, merging with another team, or at the very least, setting up a continuity plan for succession. Whatever causes you to make that move, you'll be more empowered in your choices if you start thinking ahead to that day now. Think about it so your mind is prepared. Talk about it so your family and your team are prepared.

You do not want to be an advisor who still goes into the office every day because that's all he or she knows. There is much more to life.

CHAPTER FOUR QUESTIONS

1. How deeply have you connected with your clients, your friends, your family? With your community?

2. Are you working toward a higher purpose? What is your ultimate "why?"

3. Where in your day can you find mini-impact moments? Do you have a log where you can write some of them down for reference? Even jotting them down on your calendar can be a major benefit.

4. You invest in your business, but how have you invested in your *community*?

5. How are you amplifying your platform?

CHAPTER 5

Making an Impact

*You can never have an impact on society
if you have not changed yourself.*
—Nelson Mandela

Years ago my uncle, Roland, encouraged me to join the Rotary Club where he was a member. Roland was married to my godmother—who was a major influence in my life—my aunt, Teresa. I was young, much younger than the majority of people there, and I felt like a total outcast at that first meeting. I didn't feel connected to the group, but I loved their energy. Here was a roomful of game changers—the movers and shakers in the community.

You don't just go to meetings in the Rotary Club; you have to get involved. The Italian in me made signing up for the annual spaghetti dinner an obvious choice. I grew up watching my Sicilian grandmother spend all day making the most delicious spaghetti sauce, and now I could use that knowledge in a big way.

For my participation, I had to raise $90 by selling nine tickets for $10 each. If I didn't sell them, I still had to come up with $90 to pay for those tickets. Now, that doesn't seem like a lot of money today, but joining the Rotary back then cost me $1,000 a year, which was already a large investment at the time. I was willing to stretch my budget to make it work, though, because I sensed that it was important and could lead to bigger things in my career. But those tickets were one more thing that I couldn't afford, so I sold them to nine friends and family members. I clearly remember thinking that the Rotary Club had no understanding of what young professionals deal with when it comes to finances. At least I had the dinner to look forward to.

As it turned out, I had no hand at all in making the spaghetti sauce or anything else served that evening. Still, I expected a good meal and was excited to share it with my family and friends who had ponied up ten bucks each to be there. Well, you can imagine my horror as we shuffled into a high school cafeteria for dinner. Behind the long counter, lunchroom ladies in hairnets stirred cauldrons of overcooked noodles that were utterly drowning in soupy marinara sauce. I literally mistook the sauce for cooking water; it was that thin. For all you movie aficionados, think Billy Madison's lunch lady serving sloppy joes. I was appalled and embarrassed.

I offered to help in the kitchen, thinking I could whip up a few decent plates for the people I'd sold tickets to, but I was told that I wasn't allowed behind the counter. The club had subbed out the cooking to these lovely women, who were unfortunately horrible cooks.

I ended up serving drinks, and not even good drinks. We had iced tea and lemonade. I looked around the room, thinking, *Is this the best we can do? Really?*

Maybe I was missing something. Why were so many leaders, business owners, and even city officials involved in this horrible event? It was obviously not something any of them looked forward to or even enjoyed. It was more like a duty. You were expected to be there. Thinking there must be a catch, I did the math. The ticket sales brought in nearly $10,000—a respectable amount—but after the cost of meals, drinks, site, and service, we had only about $3,000 left for charity. I couldn't believe it. Why put people through this demoralizing ordeal, when we could have raised as much or more by simply asking every Rotary member to donate $90?

Around this same time, my aunt had finished her last surgery in her battle with breast cancer, and I went to visit her and Uncle Roland. She asked me how the spaghetti dinner was, and I looked at Roland and said, "You rotten S.O.B. You knew this was going to be the crappiest dinner ever, and you let me do it anyway."

Roland laughed and said, "Why do you think I didn't go?" Well, he had me. I vented about that awful dinner for another ten minutes before my uncle stopped me.

"If it's so bad, what do you think we should do instead?" and I immediately replied, "Wine festival!"

I don't know exactly why that thought popped into my head or out of my mouth. Maybe because, at my age, I was finally graduating from beer and realizing the joys of a great glass of wine with dinner. I'd attended other festivals—Norfolk's Town Point Virginia Festival and the Neptune Wine Festival in Virginia Beach—and the experience was exhilarating. Wine, it seemed, was reaching a new dawn, and sampling it outside in the fresh air with friends and coworkers was an event whose time had arrived. The demographic at these events was much different than the fundraisers I was used to. Women outnumbered the men by a high margin, and they came in groups. For them, the wine festival was more than a social event—it was a celebration, and that festive vibe echoed through the event. Knowing the possibilities, I was confident that others would see the value and the opportunity in launching a wine festival of our own.

Our festival would be different, because it wouldn't be for profit—we'd do the whole thing for local charities. Roland sort of lit up. He wasn't 100 percent sold on the idea, but I could tell that he was intrigued. I should tell you that before this day, Roland and I had never worked together on anything, really. All my life he was my uncle—not a business partner, not a professional colleague. Our relationship in the Rotary Club had been good, but the difference between us in age and seniority had kept me from truly opening up to my uncle with my ideas. But on this day, I showed him who I was and what I believed we could do. I think Roland connected with that enthusiasm and saw me in a different light: as a strategic thinker with big ideas. That day, we bonded over the idea of a charity wine festival.

When I got home less than half an hour later, I found a bunch of emails and articles from Roland in my inbox, all about wine festivals. We were onto something. The Rotary Club was looking for new service projects, and I emailed the board my idea: *I think we should do a wine festival*, I wrote. *Here's my pitch.*

I basically told them why a wine festival made sense, and why all the tired old ideas—barbecue, oyster roast, shrimp fest—did not. Nobody seemed all that interested, but they didn't shoot it down either. In fact, my wine festival got put on a ballot, along with "barbecue."

The board meeting, where everyone voted, was held right before the member meeting, so I was standing in the parking lot when the board convened. One of the board members approached me. "You won," he said, "by one vote. And we want you to be the chairperson."

I and a half dozen others on the wine festival committee had our first meeting the next week. Roland showed up and listened in, and afterward he came up to me and said, "Do you have any idea what you're getting yourself into?"

I had a vague idea, but I was young and had that fire in my belly to make it happen. That, and the memory of that disgusting spaghetti dinner, motivated me to make the wine festival a success.

I ended up cold calling more than fifty wineries and got about half of them to agree to attend. We picked a date that fit all their calendars—no small feat—and were on our way. Putting a date on the event made it real, and Roland and I started connecting with businesses to help support it.

He and I pitched the wine festival to sponsors. We wanted $25,000 for a lead sponsor, but no one wanted to pay that much, so we didn't have a lead sponsor that first year. One business offered us $7,500, and we turned it down. Instead, we stuck to our guns and our prices, and even though we didn't have a lead sponsor, we signed up plenty of others for less money. And the next year, we sold that lead sponsorship.

That first year, twenty wineries participated and 8,000 people showed up. The wineries were all from my state, Virginia, and we also set up an international wine tasting tent with twenty wines from around the world. The other festivals didn't offer wines from other places, and I wanted an international flair so people could sample not only the best that Virginia had to offer, but wines from around the country and the world.

We netted $150,000 for charity that year, which was a club, community, and personal game changer.

You have the power to make more of an impact than you could ever imagine. With a lot of work and a lot of help, I made my dream of a wine festival that wasn't just a social event, but a charitable enterprise, a reality.

It sounds easy, reading these few paragraphs, but it was actually a lot of work. Learning how to set up a festival and dealing with all the logistics—from finding a location, to getting permits, to renting tents, and all the communication required—just about did me in, but I had help. The community came together to support the festival in a big way, from the local law enforcement to the city council and more than 400 volunteers who wanted to be a part of the event.

I learned a lot of lessons, too, like don't give your volunteers free tickets weeks before the event. Several people who got those tickets never showed up to help. Lesson learned. The other half who did show up, worked their tails off and came away with a real understanding of what it means to make an impact in their community, and ultimately, to be part of a living legacy.

THE POWER OF GENERATIONAL DIVERSITY

Joining with Roland to launch the wine festival taught me an important lesson that transferred well into other areas of my life: whatever your generation, you can benefit from working together with people who are older or younger than you.

When you're young, you often find yourself surrounded by other young people who don't have the experience, wisdom, or resources to bring your ideas to fruition. Your amazing idea, like un-harvested grapes, wither and die on the vine.

This is what happens when young people sit around sharing all their great ideas over drinks and don't seek out mentors—or anyone who's ahead of them in the lifecycle of their careers—to help them launch their ideas into actual projects. Not that younger people can't do this on their own, but it's a lot easier with help from people who've been around awhile and are willing to share their wisdom.

This goes both ways. As we get older, we get a little worn out chasing new ideas and we stop executing on them. Young people bring the energy we need to stay excited about new projects. Without them, we stop saying yes because we're all too busy and don't want to take on one more thing, even if that one thing can have a huge impact.

So whether you're a Baby Boomer or a member of Generation X, Y (Millennial), or Z, don't overlook the benefits of collaborating with people older or younger than you.

FINDING SOMETHING BIGGER THAN MYSELF

Every year, I do a debrief with everyone involved in the wine festival. We talk about the successes, the challenges, and the failures—lessons learned for the next festival. After the first event, I took a step back to reflect on how I felt about the whole thing. While the festival was a tremendous success, it wasn't without its struggles. Emotionally, the festival had taken its toll, and this was something I needed to examine more closely, with some personal introspection.

While I was planning that first event, I was also building my own financial services business. Between the business and the festival, I spread myself pretty thin, and with limited bandwidth, I focused on working behind the scenes. If I could just manage the logistics, I knew I could rely on Roland to help me with all the other activities that needed our attention: being out front meeting with people, getting our message out, and gaining community and support for the festival. As much as I appreciated all the support, his visibility resulted in—what I felt at the time—an inordinate amount of attention. I shouldn't have let this bother me, but it did. I had dedicated so much of myself to the wine festival and frankly, did not want to relinquish any control—or credit.

During that first debrief, we talked about this. Roland's take on the matter was that he was trying to help me with an unbelievably complicated project. He had time and he had connections. He knew the right people, and he really wanted the festival to succeed. I saw it another way, specifically that this wine festival was my vision, my "baby," yet it appeared to outsiders as if Roland was in charge of the whole thing. The wine festival was near and dear to my heart, and not just because it involved one of my favorite beverages. I saw it as potentially being a game changer for me, for our business, and for the community. And a small part of me didn't want to share ownership of it.

But ultimately, the result came from teamwork. One of my mantras at my practice, Freedom Street Partners, is "Better Together." I do some things better than other people, and other people do some things better than I do. Roland and I found a great chemistry, and we leveraged that chemistry to change the community for the better. This was a lesson in leadership that I haven't forgotten. As much as I wanted to own the festival, I wouldn't have wanted to do it without Roland. I don't know if I *could* have. He was the perfect COO to my CEO. While I was running the front of the house—working with the wineries, arranging the flow of guests in and out of the event, and building a brand—Roland was running the back of the house: organizing the order of events, managing electronic tickets, and ordering wrist bands. Think of a restaurant, where the front of the house is everything that the patron sees, and the back of the house is where a lot of behind-the-scenes work is accomplished. They're both equally important. Without a great back of the house—the locally sourced, fresh ingredients and masterful chef—the food can still be delivered by the best server in the world at the fanciest eatery, but no one will want to eat it. My wine festival vision would have been nothing without someone on the execution side who believed in it from the beginning. In hindsight, I realized that the credit didn't matter. What truly mattered was the outcome: the money we raised and what we did with it.

That first year, within seven days of the event, we wrote checks to local charities. Ten years later, with ten successful wine festivals under my belt, we've donated over $2 million to local charities. We've also hosted spring festivals to raise money. Another benefit of the event was motivating the city to improve the park for the wine festival and other events, adding a concert stage, amphitheater, raised lawns, a graded setting, greenery, sidewalks, and walking paths. Other groups around the country have contacted us for assistance with their wine festivals, and we've created a ripple effect that's helped raise more money than I will ever know. Many of them do a wine festival only once, because they don't know going into it how much work is involved. But that doesn't take anything away from the single event, and what they accomplish with it.

Hundreds of thousands of dollars that we've raised have gone to the Boys & Girls Clubs of America and to the Sidney M. Oman Cancer Treatment Center at our local hospital, Chesapeake Regional Medical Center. Our festival's funds made us one of the lead sponsors of a mobile mammogram unit for women in our area. We've also donated money to support Honor and Remember, which gives flags to the families of fallen soldiers. We paid for a dentist's chair in a clinic so that homeless people and others can get free dental care.

Seeing this kind of impact energizes me to keep going every year. No matter how much work it takes, I never question if what I'm doing is worth all the effort. Aside from all the good the wine festival has done in my community, it's created a spark in me. I want to do better every year, and I believe we *can* do better. That spark drives me and surrounds me with people who have the same belief. The event gives me a purpose that's bigger than myself. I may never be able to write a personal check for $1 million to my favorite charity, but by partnering with others, I've been able to raise a lot of money for people who need it in a very short amount of time.

The wine festival lit a spark in Roland, too, and he went on to run for city council—and won. He's made our community a better place in that role. He still supports the annual wine festival from behind the scenes, and I know I can count on him for any other support when I need it; likewise, I will always be there for him. Roland and I will always be a championship team—like a Belichick and Brady for Charity, or a Dallas Cowboys fan, a Jimmy Johnson, Troy Aikman.

What does all of this mean for you? Well, I believe you're no different than I am. Like me, you love being an advisor, but want more. You want your life to mean something. You want a sense of purpose beyond everything you do for your clients, family, and friends, and you know you can do more. You want to create a legacy that you can start living right now, not to be remembered by when you're dead and gone, unable to enjoy it every single day.

> *Never get so busy making a living*
> *that you forget to make a life.*
> —Dolly Parton

My wife Adrienne and I enjoying the fruits of labor: a glass of wine at the annual wine festival.

Have you ever been to a funeral or a memorial? We say such wonderful things about people who have passed on. Too bad they don't get to hear any of it. Those words aren't about what the person did at work, either—they're about who the person was, how they lived their life, and what they did for the world. If you want people to talk about you this way before your funeral, start creating your legacy today.

I had a moment, when I was working on the festival, when I wondered if it would help my career. I admit it—that was a self-serving thought, but I'm human. I worried that maybe I was putting in all this time for nothing, because it wouldn't do anything for the business. What a stupid thought. Of course, after the first one, I realized how short-sighted I had been. My career wasn't what mattered in the big scheme of things. What mattered was everything the festival did for everyone else involved, everyone who volunteered or attended, and everyone who benefitted from the money we raised. I could see the festival as something bigger for me—the start of actually *living* what's important to me, building a legacy that would outshine anything I could do as a business owner.

And, in fact, it did affect my career. People who had never talked to me in the past, who saw me in one role, now saw me in an entirely new light. They believed in what I was doing and wanted to help. They wanted to associate with me. They saw me differently, and I saw them differently too. I saw them as people who cared about our city and the people in it, and not simply as potential clients.

I've met other advisors who have begun living their legacies in various ways. You don't have to do it with a wine festival, but you can find a way to lend your own special talents and passion to create something that makes a positive impact in your community.

The key is not to wait. Don't hold off until you're too busy or too tired, or you have too many obligations to start something. Start something now. Start small, test out your ideas, find the right people to build it with you, and watch it grow.

You may never know your total impact. What began as my dissatisfaction with a spaghetti dinner blossomed into the Chesapeake Wine Fest. That event spawned so much goodwill and so many changes for my community—and other communities—that I can't quantify it.

There were indirect benefits, too, like the media coverage and professional and community awards and accolades; I also met people whom I've since worked with professionally. But if that had been my goal, I'm convinced that I would have failed. Another unexpected result was the influx of diversity in our Rotary Club. Our membership had new life. It was younger, and more women than ever were interested in joining in the mission of the club that had so long been populated by a male majority. And Roland and I have gone on to consult on other clubs' events, including one in Virginia that's donated more than $1 million to local charities.

Approach your legacy for the right reason: to do something good in the world with no expectations. Don't expect anything in return. Don't even expect to control the result. You have to go into this with an open heart, wanting to do some good with no strings attached—not even the expectation that you will feel good about yourself. A gift is a gift, and it must be presented as such, for the benefit of the recipient.

THE HABIT OF MAKING AN IMPACT

A longtime friend whom I hadn't spoken with in years called me one morning for advice. I had a pile of work on my desk, and it would have been easy for me to tell him I was too busy to talk. That thought *did* cross my mind. But I try to never be too busy for someone who needs my help, so I spent forty-five minutes on the phone with him, giving him guidance to get his business on track. If he had called just to shoot the breeze (or to procrastinate from doing any work, which some advisors are prone to do), our conversation might have been shorter. I believe, however, that when you are given an opportunity to make a difference in someone's life, you should view it as a gift, and honor that gift. It meant getting a little behind on my own work, but I knew right away that this friend needed my help.

If I focused solely on billable hours, my impact in the world would be limited. All too often, people who have much to give hold back because they want to know what's in it for them. I can't tell you how many people I know who have joined service organizations and quit within a year because they didn't feel like they were getting their money's worth. If you ask these people what they gave of themselves, they have to think about it. If all they gave was the membership dues, that's not enough.

Years ago I read Gary Chapman's *The Five Love Languages*, and one of the "aha" moments in that book for me was (paraphrased) "If you're not receiving the affection you crave, look in the mirror: How are you showing affection?"[7] That code of reciprocity stuck with me, and I've leveraged it not only in my personal life, but in business as well. Basically, if you want to be treated better, treat others better. If you want something, first give something. Even John Lennon and Paul McCartney said, in the Beatles' final recorded song "The End": "And in the end, the love you take is equal to the love you make."

If you want more love and affection, show more love and affection. If you want people to make you dinner, make *them* dinner. If you want your children to respect you better,

7   Gary Chapman, *The 5 Love Languages: The Secret to Love that Lasts* (Chicago: Northfield, 2015).

show a higher level of respect for them. Having an impact starts with the little things you do each day that can have a dramatic impact beyond what you see in the moment. You cannot put a dollar value on changing a person's life. When you put your hand out, have something in it to give. You'll be amazed by what you might get back. I work on this behavior daily, because knowing what's right doesn't always lead to doing what's right. It takes work, and awareness.

When a man is guided by the principles of reciprocity and consciousness, he is not far from the moral law. Whatever you don't wish for yourself don't do unto others.
—Confucius

In chapter 3, I told you about breaking a habit by identifying the cue and focusing on fixing that, rather than the symptom, such as biting your fingernails. This is from Charles Duhigg's book *The Power of Habit*. Just like breaking a bad habit, you can create a good habit, such as the habit of making an impact.

What you do has far greater impact than what you say.
—Stephen Covey

Building a habit of impact means giving to other people on a regular basis without expectation and judgment. To develop this habit, you have to be open and aware of opportunities to give in this way. The more opportunities you become aware of, and respond to, the more you will begin to get back.

FOLLOW YOUR PASSION

Making an impact and creating a legacy is easy and much more fun if it's based on whatever you're passionate about. I knew what made me happy: serving people, planning and throwing events, and wine. When I tied them all together, the wine festival was born.

That first year, I was a sponsor too—figured I had to be if I was going to get other people onboard. Remember, I was young and wasn't exactly rolling in the dough, but I was willing to invest a thousand dollars of my own money in the event. In that way, by "putting my money where my mouth was," I could talk to people without feeling like I was asking for a handout—I was inviting them to join me in an event that had the potential to make a real difference in our community.

I still make a financial contribution every year by sponsoring the tickets. Our business is on the back of every ticket sold for the event, so in addition to combining all my other passions, I've been able to squeeze my work into the festival too. I will tell you, when you can combine everything you love about your life—the work, the people, and the passions—you've hit your sweet spot.

Discovering how to make an impact can be as simple as finding the intersection between your business, your relationships, and your passion, and building something that unifies all of them.

Think about that for yourself. What do you love about your work? What are you passionate about? Whom do you care about and want to help? How can you tie those together to make an impact that gets you excited and *means* something? If you can figure that out, you've found your purpose in life, and you can make an impact right now and in the future. You can create a living legacy.

As you're building this legacy, your platform grows. The larger your stage gets, the more room there is to invite others to join you. Then, not only does your impact grow exponentially, but the people who choose to join you will also experience what you're feeling—the joy of making a positive difference in the world.

For the wine festival, we set up "corporate chalets" which are large tents that companies sponsor so their people have a place to gather. Between 80 and 90 percent of the sponsors return every year, and we get new sponsors to reserve the remaining chalets. Inviting people from other businesses onto your stage makes it easy and fun for them to share in the impact you're making.

The wine festival is special in that the majority of our sponsors are businesses. Since people are there with their families and coworkers, there's accountability and sheer ownership for the success of the event. Everyone has a good time together while making an impact for the community. It's a terrific opportunity to meet people and build relationships that continue long after the event ends.

WEATHERING STORMS

Giving without expectation is one of many lessons the wine festival taught me. I also learned a lot of business lessons, because I was rubbing shoulders with some very successful people in the community. I had to learn how to respectfully navigate the room so to speak, giving people roles without making them feel diminished, backing down at times to empower others to make decisions, and stepping in to call the shots when necessary.

I learned how to deal with the adversity that comes with working with many people, and with more obvious adversity—like weather. Twice we held the festival on the day of a hurricane, and twice a nor'easter threatened to take down the event. When Hurricane Sandy created a state of emergency, we opened the gates at noon, just as the wind picked up and the rain began. We were lucky—the gusts weren't strong enough to tear down our tents or shut down the event. There was plenty of backlash just the same; on social media, some people questioned our judgment: *How could you host a wine festival at a time like this?* I suspect the backlash would have been just as severe if we had canceled. Nevertheless, 6,000 people showed up, and we raised a lot of money.

You can't control everything—especially the weather. I found that out when storms threatened the wine festival.

Hurricane Matthew was worse. Even though it wasn't supposed to hit our area, I spent the week prior putting together a contingency plan, and I almost canceled it. The wine festival is a rain or shine event, meaning the money for the tickets has been collected and there are no refunds. Then the weather report changed, and it looked like we might get a taste of the storm in the late afternoon. I moved the event up an hour to eleven o'clock and held my breath. Well, Matthew hit right on schedule from the south, colliding with a nor'easter from the north, and delivering a much worse storm than anyone expected. We lasted until four o'clock, when lightning shut us down. We got everyone out, and I remember standing in three feet of water and hurricane wind gusts, trying to salvage the tents that were getting torn apart. We and our partners lost forty tents in the storm, but we netted $100,000 for charity.

You will deal with hurricanes in business, in your personal life, and when you're trying to make an impact too. But if you have the right people around you, processes in place, and a contingency plan, you will weather a lot of storms and still manage to find a lot of success.

YOU DON'T KNOW YOU CAN MAKE A DIFFERENCE UNTIL YOU DO

All this sounds a little overwhelming, right? Remember, when I started, I knew nothing at all about wine festivals, or tents, or what hurricanes do to wine festivals and tents. I hadn't even thought about it—why would I? If I had thought about it too much and focused on all the things that could go wrong, I never would have done anything. I would still be thinking about how I'm getting closer to retirement, and how—outside of what I do for my family, friends, and clients—I've made no real impact on the world, or even in my community. I certainly wouldn't be writing this book.

So much of what we do seems to make no difference at all. Then there are those moments when we realize that something we did or said actually *did* make a difference. Think about all the times you told your kids to eat their vegetables, or brush their teeth, or not get into debt. It feels like everything you say falls on deaf ears, until you actually see them follow your advice or model your behavior. You might even catch them repeating your advice to someone else. That little twinge you get—knowing you made a positive impact on another person's life—feels so good. Now imagine making a positive impact on the lives of dozens, hundreds, or even thousands of people.

> *We are what we repeatedly do. Excellence,*
> *then, is not an act, but a habit.*
> —Aristotle

Like Nike says, "Just Do It." Not "Just Try It." Trying is dabbling. It's not giving your best effort. Effort comes from *doing*. Don't worry about being polished or perfect, especially at first. It's going to be awkward, and clumsy, and difficult. But as long as it's *you*, that's okay. Don't copy what everyone else is doing. Figure out what's unique about you, because that's what you and only you can bring to the world. Believe it, and go forward, and don't worry about failing because as long as you're doing something good and putting your energy behind whatever it is you're passionate about, you will have an impact.

You're going to question your qualifications, and so will a lot of other people. It's like being a new advisor. Remember when you were brand new in this business and everyone looked at you like you didn't know a thing? You were a rookie, a novice, a "noob."

I don't feel like anyone really believed we could pull off a wine festival. I had to find the confidence to not care about what other people thought about me, knowing that if I kept pushing through, with a lot of passion (not to mention on-the-job training), I would somehow succeed. Instead of focusing on pleasing the naysayers, put all that energy into doing what you believe is right for you and your community. Prove them wrong, then ask them to join you.

If I followed the advice of everyone who didn't believe in me over the years, I would never accomplish anything. People told me that leaving my job as an employee of a great financial firm to start my own business was dumb. People told me that advisors don't need help from other advisors, they just need to do their own thing. People even told me I would never write a book. Those people were all wrong. I love our business, and I loved writing this book.

And between doing those two things, I learned that advisors do need help and guidance. I've watched too many of them struggle to sit back and pretend those other people—the ones who didn't believe what I did—were right. So many advisors don't know what they should be doing now, or what they're going to be doing when they come to their retirement. I want to help them.

CHAPTER FIVE QUESTIONS

1. Do you have a daily routine? What does it look like?
    Is it built around making an impact?

2. Do you surround yourself with people who are
    younger and provide you with more energy?

3. Are you surrounding yourself with wiser people that
    have developed things that you want to develop?
    Who is your mentor?

4. When you talk about impact, what kind of impact do
    you want to make? Is it localized to your own family?
    Is it something outside or bigger than yourself?

5. What's your wine festival? Is there something that
    you're doing that's creating a wave for other orga-
    nizations or people in your community?

6. What are some of the things you're doing every year
    and not even thinking about, but if you were writing
    them down it would really be making a large impact
    in your life? Are you inventorying those things?

CHAPTER 6

Living Your Legacy

What you leave behind is not what is engraved in the stone monuments, but what is woven into the lives of others.
—Pericles

Soon after starting my financial career at one of the biggest firms in the country, I discovered how much I enjoyed talking with the new people. Even then, I realized that helping other advisors gave me as much satisfaction as helping clients. Mentoring, coaching—these were my lanes, and I leaned in hard, at times even sacrificing management's leanings to assist a colleague. Being that helper, that guide, spoke to my deepest instincts and led me down the path of coach and mentor from six months into the business through years of learning, practice, and fine-tuning my skills, right up to the present.

Mary was one of many advisors I've worked with over the years. She had been through the excellent training program offered by our employer, but she was struggling in the field. Determined to succeed, Mary returned to the home office to repeat her training. As she was finishing up this second round, Mary came to me for advice. She was considering transferring to another office where the company believed she might have a better chance of success, but inside, she wanted to stay put and figure out the job, no matter how difficult it might be.

She asked me about that other office—*was it really as good as everyone was saying?*

I asked her, "How do you feel about it, and how does your family feel about it?"

"I don't know," she said. "My husband doesn't want to move. He's in school and doing well, and most of my family is here. But everyone at work keeps telling me what a great opportunity it is. I just don't know what to think."

I couldn't lie to Mary or give her anything less than my best advice; I believed she needed another chance, but she also needed someone to believe in her. When you don't find immediate success at a job, it can be difficult to find allies. People tend to distance themselves from you and even quit on you—often unintentionally or even unconsciously, and maybe for career survival. Was this Mary's experience? I don't know. But I did think she wasn't getting the best advice for *her*.

I said, "Moving to that other office may be a great opportunity financially, but relocating your family is a big decision. Think about where you want your life to be. If you're just following the money, you could end up very unhappy with your decision. Where do you want to live? If it's here, then make it happen here. I believe you can do it."

Mary stayed, and she turned out to be very good at her job. We've been friends ever since, and I still mentor her.

People like Mary reinforced in me the value of having the integrity to tell people the truth—even when it's not what everyone else is telling them, and even when it's not what they want to hear.

ADVISOR TO MENTOR

Other advisors came to me for advice, and the more I mentored them, the more I realized how many advisors struggled with making decisions like this—decisions that had a dramatic effect on their lives.

This really bothered me. It kept me up at night, and I wanted to do something about it. So I came up with this mission: to teach other advisors how to use the skills they already have to make decisions, and take actions today that give them a bright future tomorrow.

I started with the advisors around me—the people I worked with. And as I mentored them, I discovered something else. Helping these people didn't only make their lives better, it also helped them become better advisors for their clients. I was enhancing the lives of people I hadn't even met—more clients than I could have ever reached on my own!

Then I noticed something else: helping others made *my* life better. A lot better. I expanded on this concept and figured out a way to make a real impact not only for advisors and their clients, but for my entire community. This part of the legacy I was creating, with the help from my friends, would likely outlive me. And I didn't have to wait to retire to do it.

I went from being a financial advisor focused on the happenings on Wall Street to being a valued member of my family, my team, and my community, living a richer life, creating a legacy, and owning my future. I went from Wall Street to Freedom Street.

THE BIG SHIFT

I came out of 2007 feeling good about myself and my work. After year upon year of significant, continued growth, I felt like I had a real business and a solid base of clients. I had made the shift from "hustler" to advisor and was becoming a true financial consultant. A lot of things were changing for the better: I was shifting from the old world of day-to-day transactions to the new world of financial planning and consulting. The stars were aligned. I could see the future and it was bright. Nothing, it seemed, could stand in my way.

Then 2008 happened, and it was a whole new ballgame. Due to the economic downturn, people were suffering, and I felt their pain. Advisors I was training were questioning their career choice. I had just shifted to a business model that was better for my clients, but where my paydays would be later and stretched out over longer periods of time. This was the worst possible time to transition a business. But the alternative—waking up hungry for the next "deal" every day—wasn't sustainable, and it wasn't what I wanted for our business. I had to move away from that kind of hunger toward a hunger to build a business that served clients in a different capacity.

The year 2008 was a real eye-opener for a lot of investors and advisors. It was hard not to focus on what was wrong. I could have gone that route, dwelling on the economy and worrying about what *else* could go wrong. Despite all the bad stuff going on in the world, the industry, and my life, I turned my focus away from what was going wrong and imagined what was possible.

This was a tough time, but it's often in those tough times when being true to yourself and what you believe is most important. My wife was pregnant with our second child, so I was feeling the stress at home. I had to be there for her and for our family. I was feeling it at work, too, because people were worried.

The market was losing value, which was affecting *everyone*. You did what was best for your clients, but in times of adversity and market downs, even your best can be quite challenging. You hope you've made the right choices for people, especially regarding their exposure to risk, knowing it's still going to be rough going for a while. And through all this, you have to stay positive. People are looking to you to be that rock, that beacon of light in the darkness. So I kept pushing through and running the business the way I believed it should be run. I remember saying to my wife after a particularly trying day, "This is either the end of my career or the beginning of a really great opportunity for us."

We were actually—of all things—house shopping at the time. Like we could afford to be looking at a bigger mortgage. It was very uncomfortable, and a little bit scary.

But whenever I've had that feeling, like I'm maybe a little close to the edge, a breakthrough follows.

What followed was that I joined the Rotary Club and shifted my mindset from "this could be the end," to "this is a great beginning." I found time to give time to others. I found time to read every business book I could get my hands on, and I learned to run my practice better. I read books by Steve Moeller, Matt Oechsli, and Nick Murray, looking for practices that were superior to those of the traditional model of a financial services company. Then I thought about how to transfer those teachings to my own practice. I was already on the right track with the right intentions and mindset, but I was looking to fill in any gaps in my knowledge to build the best model to serve my clients.

In a time when I could have crumpled under the pressure, I found the strength and focus to make it work. Of course, my wife had a lot to do with that at home, and my work team had a lot to do with that at my practice. I got plenty of support for the wine festival too. As long as I stood by my purpose and kept showing up, I knew in my heart it would somehow work out.

By 2010, with a growing family and a growing business, I could see the light at the end of the tunnel. I had cracked through a plateau of mediocrity and was up 56 percent in pure production. But then I hit a wall, and I brought in a junior advisor. People told me this was a dumb move—it was too early and I didn't have the assets. But my thought was, *If I can get down to 100–115 households of high-quality relationships, I can really grow this business.*

Undaunted, I also hired a business coach, Steve Moeller, that year. He had the words to describe what I was doing with our business, and he knew how to take it even further. We talked about interviewing clients and going deeper to understand what really matters to them. This is when I began to feel less like an advisor and more of a consultant to my clients—like a life coach who specialized in money. I did investment management, scenario planning, and vision coaching. Steve helped me lay out my goals and dial in my processes. The investment I made in his training, along with the investment I made in the business, are what propelled me to the next level.

My wife and I finally bought our new house that year, too. For me, everything really was coming together. I felt like I had finally gotten out of my own way. The possibilities were endless.

GET OUT OF YOUR OWN WAY

To me, "get out of your own way" means to *stop over-thinking everything in the business and understand that other people know better than you.* I had to hire a coach who wasn't afraid to point out when I was BSing myself. As self-reliant and self-confident as I am, I needed that confidante who could look at me and my business from the outside and tell me the truth. He and I saw things the same way, which I needed, because the old way I'd learned to do business didn't work, and I knew it. But he could see through a lot of what I could not—some of the old ways I had hung onto that didn't serve me anymore. In a way, he gave me that extra boost, too, to go with my gut and do what I knew was right.

The business exploded that year, but it didn't overwhelm me because I had put structure around it, scaled smart, and made the growth manageable. Building up the business had required working long days, week after week, and I had to curb those hours back to a normal workweek. I figured out how to take the month of July off, essentially, which I still aim to do every year. I scheduled all my review appointments before June 25th, my birthday. Then I'd attend the company's regional meeting before going on vacation. But I didn't just disappear for all of July; we took family vacations for parts of the month, and for other parts, I worked most mornings but kept afternoons and weekends for myself and my family. This was the annual hard reset I needed to decompress and get a little bit of distance, so that by August I could come back full-time, refreshed.

When you start focusing on building something bigger than yourself, like a business, a family, or a community event, you don't have time to focus on the stupid stuff that can clutter up your day and your head. Trivial stuff, and anything that's beyond your control, doesn't grab your attention. Your focus is directed on what you're building.

You don't have to wait for the worst of times to get out of your own way. Anytime is the best time to do it. I just happened to do it around one of the worst recessions in my lifetime, but even when everything seems to be going well, there is opportunity for exponential improvement and growth. In business, our success is often right in front of us: our current client, our current staff, the current opportunity, that thing we're really great at that nobody else is. It's right in front of us, but we don't see it, and we start looking for that magic pill that will solve all our problems.

There's no perfect time to transform your business and your life, and there's no perfect time to start living your legacy. There is no one perfect time to exit the business, either. Some people look to market returns for that answer, while others believe you should look at your family, your life, and the world, and let those be your guide. There is no right or wrong answer. The key is to get in front of it and take control. Most people delay the decision until they're forced to make it, which is rarely the best time, because by then you have less control over the timeline. Whether your life, your business, or the markets are up or down doesn't matter if you can't choose your own timeline. Put aside what you can't control and focus on what you can.

PAYING IT FORWARD

During the economic downturn, investors and advisors were sort of paralyzed. My region's advisors were among the top performers, and since I was coaching them, leadership wanted to understand the differentiator—what were we doing that other regions were not?

I remember thinking, *Gosh, how lucky am I?* I had the best group of young advisors I could have ever dreamed of, and they listened to me. They didn't need to experience failure for themselves before they executed on what I told them to do. They listened, they believed, and they acted. They were the perfect students, and during one of the roughest financial times, they thrived. On the other hand, I also had advisors who weren't doing as well with the transition. Several were really struggling with consistency because their success often relied on the success of the market. In 2008, you can imagine how that was going for them. Some were under-producing so badly that the company was preparing to let them go. These advisors were so broken that they couldn't get out of their own way.

One guy in particular I remember well. He had started the same time as I had, but he was about to be fired. One of the head trainers referred him to me. "I think you can help him," she said. When I met Andy, all he wanted to talk about was the business and how bad everything was. I had to pull him out of that thinking and get him on track with what mattered in life. I had to get him out of his head.

I asked him, "Can you just tell me what's most important in your life right now?" That shifted the conversation immediately.

"Well," he said, "my son's a high school senior and he's getting ready to go to college and play baseball, but with everything I have on my plate, I cannot even fathom getting away to see him play."

"Okay, what else?" I asked.

He told me about a pumpkin patch that he ran with his family for a couple of months in the fall. It was his favorite time of the year.

I said, "Do you see how you feel when you talk about your son, your family, your pumpkin patch? That's what matters. And we can work with the rest. If you're open minded and willing to listen, I can coach you. But I won't listen to you complain about these things that are out of our control."

I worked with Andy and showed him how to make all the transitions I had made, moving to a service-based model, not shying away from his clients and wallowing in the negative, but digging in to be there for them even more. Over the next year, he joined in my group coaching sessions and flew out several times for one-on-one coaching. I also connected Andy with other coaches who were skilled in particular topics where he needed help.

The next year, he was at every one of his kid's baseball games. He hired a second assistant in his office. Andy had been stuck in a rut, unable to get out of his own way. Once he focused on what he could change about his situation, he did, and for the better.

FOUR QUADRANTS OF LIFE

I used to always keep one of those big paper calendars on my desk. Sure, I had my Outlook calendar too, but the activities on online calendars tend to disappear. They get checked off or deleted, and the days get moved into the past and out of sight. Paper calendars have a way of preserving history. They also help me feel more productive every day because I can see everything I accomplished.

At the end of the year, I'd flip through that calendar to remind myself of everything I'd accomplished—all the productivity, even some of the fun. There was so much detail, and it not only reminded me of all that I'd done, it showed me how crazy life could get when I was trying to do too much and not focusing on what was most important.

One day when I was feeling kind of overwhelmed at work, I tore one of those big pages from my desk calendar. I flipped it over to the blank side and wrote down everything that was weighing on my mind—not the day-to-day stuff, but the things that were really bugging me. This was the important stuff that I felt like I should be paying attention to but maybe wasn't. If I just did a big brain dump and got it all on paper, maybe it wouldn't be so overwhelming.

Instead of just scribbling a list of to-do's, I wanted to focus on the most important concerns in my life. I drew two lines on the paper, one vertically and the other horizontally, dividing the page into four quadrants. Then I wrote in each square: FAMILY, WORK, SPIRITUALITY, HEALTH.

Under FAMILY I wrote everything I wanted to do for my wife, kids, and all my relatives: (1) Register Bobby for soccer; (2) Start planning family vacation; (3) Talk with Adrienne about this ... My parents need that ... Set this up with my nieces ... and so on. Everything around family that was racing around in my head went on that list. I did the same for the other three quadrants: WORK, SPIRITUALITY, and HEALTH.

You're probably already doing something like this for work, right? You have everything you need to do on a task list or a calendar, and those are the to-do's that tend to get done. Work, for me, had many subcategories: community events, boards, etc. Making lists for the other parts of my life helped me move my focus away from work and got me to pay attention to areas of my life that were just as important, if not *more* important.

FAMILY	WORK
• Plan date nights with Adrienne • Register Bobby for soccer • Start planning family vacation • Discuss estate plan with my parents	• Senior management meetings at home office for future growth • Org chart review with consultant • Prep for call cycle and client relationship management • Prep for taxes • Hire two new advisors
SPIRITUALITY	**HEALTH**
• Meditate for ten minutes daily • Meet with Pastor on fundraising • Morning prayer • Daily journal on gratitude	• Schedule annual visits with concierge doctor • Regular cryotherapy • Schedule massages • Schedule personal training sessions three months out

Life can get so busy that what's most important can easily be neglected. Identifying the four quadrants that matter most to you can help you to refocus.

Your quadrants could be different than mine, or they could be similar. People tend to value the same things, like family and health. If you're not a religious or spiritual person, you can replace "spirituality" with "higher purpose" instead. That quadrant is about serving something bigger than yourself.

There's a proverb that says, "A person who has their health has a thousand wishes. A person that does not has only one" (Unknown, from Jerusalem). If you're not well, health is all you can think about; when you have your health, you don't even think about it. Health is important to everyone I know, yet it's often the first priority to go when we have too much on our plates. Running late? We'll just skip that early run. Had a tough morning at work? Forget about the gym and that nice salad planned for lunch. We'll order in some fast food and eat at our desks. We don't have the time. It doesn't matter in the long run, right? But you and I know that isn't true, and if we don't take care of our health now, we'll be paying for it later!

I didn't always prioritize my health, but after making that list, I did. There was power in writing down the words, seeing them every day, and reminding myself why I wrote them. I thought about all the things I needed to change to improve and maintain my health, and little by little I started doing them. I wrote down goals for working out, stretching, and meditating. This didn't happen overnight. I had a goal of daily meditation for three years before I actually started! But I began making headway. I got the engine going by writing it down, and now I prioritize my health every day.

Spirituality had become less of a priority, unfortunately, and that was not how I was raised. I went to Catholic school, and my faith had always been there for me. During the toughest times in my life, kneeling down, saying a prayer, and having that quiet time had given me the strength and the resolution to keep going. Each time I made an important decision about my career, I would go to morning or midday mass. When I started my own business, I went to church right after breakfast. I knelt down under the Virgin Mary, lit candles, and prayed.

Many times when I'm in disarray, I realize that I've gotten away from my spirituality. I've forgotten to be grateful for all that I have, and instead, I think about what I'm trying to get. I focus on areas of my life that pull me away from what I know in my heart is most important. My spirituality quadrant needs to be filled, and so I ask myself, "Am I active right now in something more important than me? Am I acknowledging that it's more important than me? Am I taking time to pray? Am I taking time to be grateful?" The answer isn't always what I want to hear, so I have to reset and make the conscious choice to put more spirituality in my life.

Writing everything in those quadrants allowed me to see what I needed to do, and I prioritized from there. I could see the big rocks that weren't being taken care of, and that made me question where I was spending my time. Was I spinning my wheels on something that didn't matter? What decisions could I make to move the needle in each quadrant?

Sometimes, the decision is simple. For my health, I needed to work out regularly. When I go to the gym every day, I also watch what I eat. Working out makes me want to eat healthy and get enough sleep, instead of filling up on junk food and staying up late.

FIND YOUR DEEPER WHY

Beyond the four quadrants, living your legacy means helping others outside of yourself and your family, friends, colleagues, and clients. There are many, many more people whose lives you can impact for the better. Serving these people may not seem as satisfying as helping out those within your inner circle, and you may never even see the benefits. That's part of the grace of giving without expectation, though, and while you may not see the outcomes your work produces, it will change who you are inside for the better.

This part of living your legacy can be anything you choose to do, but it will mean more to you and you'll work harder to create it if it's tied to who you are inside and what drives you. This "why" goes deeper than the whys that drive your day-to-day goals, and even deeper than your four quadrants. It may not be obvious, and you may not even be aware of it or know where it comes from. Some quiet time and a lot of introspection may be needed to discover that *one thing*—an emotional experience that acted as a catalyst, forcing you in one direction or another. This defining moment might have affected you then and influenced you to become the person you are today.

When I started writing this book, I wasn't aware of that deeper why at all, but this journey—asking myself *why* I was writing this book, *why* helping clients and advisors is so important to me, *why* guiding people to a safe place in life matters—brought back a memory that answered all those questions: the memory of the intruder that broke into my house and attacked the babysitter. That memory was painful and difficult, but I believe that over the years, I had dealt with the trauma by learning to manage my mindset and calm my fears. Now, as an adult, I was in a position to help people when they needed me. Once I had mastered that ability, my outlook was brighter, more positive.

It's hard not to contrast the darkness, fear, and solitude of that night with the wine festival, which is the polar opposite. Surrounded by people, feeling safe and having fun in the sunshine might somehow be my response to that experience. Whether that's true I can't say for sure, but I do believe that my legacy and yours should be tied to something deeper than the day-to-day goals of your business and your life.

REBALANCE, REFOCUS

We all know, deep down, what's important. We all get pulled in other directions, and our focus shifts. It can happen without us even realizing it, and suddenly we're spending all our time on things that, if we're being honest, are just not that critical.

Take time to think about what's important to you. Make the decisions that need to be made to shift your time and your love into the quadrants that need you—and that you need. Having all those big rocks under control frees up your mind and opens you up to all the opportunities around you to make an impact in small ways. Think about the experiences in your life that have shaped who you are, too, and how you might draw on them to discover a legacy that's meaningful and deep.

WHY IT MATTERS

When it comes to that next chapter for you, why does living richly matter? Why should you care about making an impact? Why are we talking about taking an inventory? These should all be familiar topics, because we talk about them every day with our clients.

When you meet with a client, you want to know where they are today, where they want to be tomorrow, and how they are going to get there. It's the same in your own life: *Where do you want to be in the next stage?*

In the next part, Owning Your Future, we'll talk about how you get there.

CHAPTER SIX QUESTIONS

1. Referring to your four quadrants, answer the following questions:

    a. **Family:**

    - In his book *Vivid Vision*, Cameron Herald describes a vivid vision as "a detailed, three- to four-page document that lays out a clear, logical vision of what your company will look like in three years."[8] You may have a vivid vision for your company, but do you have one for your family?

    - What will your family look like a year from now? Do you have children going to college? A spouse who's changing careers?

    - Think about how your family is changing and how that will play out in the coming years. Then ask yourself, "What am I doing to prepare for the changes?"

    b. **Work:**

    - Do you love what you do?

    - What can you do more of—and less of—in a day?

    - Whom do you need to spend more time learning from?

    c. **Spirituality:**

    - Are you fulfilled?

    - What grounds you?

    - Are you in tune with God and/or nature?

---

8   Cameron Herald, *Vivid Vision: A Remarkable Tool For Aligning Your Business Around a Shared Vision of the Future* (Austin: Lioncrest, 2018).

d. **Health**:

- Do you like the way you feel? Do you like the way you look?

- Are you happy with your current level of physical activity? Are you doing the right exercises? Are you eating the right foods?

- Are you happy with your doctor?

- What are your health goals for the next year? Five years? Ten? What is your plan to reach these health goals?

- Should you be meditating? Why or why not?

- Are you the best version of yourself?

PART II ACTION PLAN

1. Identify the commonalities in your life between your business and your relationships outside of the business. Think about how you can use your platform to leverage those common denominators and build your community while living a life that allows you to create your legacy.

2. A good way to identify whether you're a prophet or a god is to disconnect from your business for a while. Can it run without you? Without you checking in? Without you calling every day? Without you emailing? If you separate for a week, will the business run without you? Will it survive? Are you the prophet or the god? If you find that you're the god, actions must be taken to create scalability and repeatability. Processes and systems must be put in place to allow it to operate without you. Do this: Take a day off, a week, two weeks. Stretch yourself. If you think you can take a day off, take a week, and if you think you can take a week, take two. See what happens.

3. Lay out the four quadrants and go through the exercise. Circle the areas that you have the most under control; highlight the areas that you'd like to work on the most.

PART III

Owning Your Future

The best way to find yourself,
is to lose yourself in the service of others.
—Mahatma Gandhi

When I began my career, I admired the top producers and the businesses they had built. But for many, business was the center of their universe. Work defined them. The truly successful ones, in my eyes, were more than financial advisors. They hung out with their families on the weekends, coached Pee Wee football, and took Salsa lessons with their wives. These advisors read books that weren't only about business. They had interests, friends, and hobbies outside of work, and they traveled for fun. I admired the top producers, but I wanted to define my career on something more.

CHAPTER 7

Taking Stock

YOUR CURRENT STATE
AND FUTURE POTENTIAL

The will to win, the desire to succeed,
the urge to reach your full potential...these are the keys
that will unlock the door to personal excellence.
—Confucius

In the introduction to this book, I told you it's never too late to do something about your life, your legacy, or your future. I believe that.

But when time and circumstances force us to make a decision, it's harder to decide. We feel rushed. We don't have the luxury of time to weigh all our options, and those options may be more limited than they were a couple of years ago. This is why we need to take stock now of where we are and how that affects where we could be in the future. Then we can make decisions on our own timelines, with more options and more time to consider and compare them, leading to better results. Depending on how long you wait, this isn't always the case.

Advisors Jack and Tom thought, as many of us do, that they had all the time in the world. Of course, none of us does, and depending on how long we wait and how much time we have left, our exit strategy outcomes can be quite different.

JACK

Jack came to me and my team when he was in his late seventies and looking to sell his practice. He had done almost everything right: Before we met with him, he had done a valuation and hired a company to represent his business for sale. Our company was on the list of prospective buyers for Jack to consider (along with more than thirty other companies). We qualified in the first round, so we made a formal offer. From all the offers Jack received, he decided whom he wanted to interview on the phone, and then eventually meet face-to-face. By the time we sat down with Jack, he had narrowed the list down to a handful of opportunities.

His vetting process was methodical. He used the formal offer letter to eliminate a lot of buyers whose offers didn't satisfy his financial requirements. On the phone interviews, he got to know the people he'd be handing his clients off to. He also asked a lot of questions about our process—how would we be managing his book of clients and the people his company represented?

The face-to-face meeting was, for me, the really interesting part. This is where my team not only had an opportunity to show Jack why we were his best option, it also gave us the chance to see if we were a good fit.

Jack had been an advisor for more than thirty years. He was highly successful, and his business had been doing over a million dollars of production. When we met, he was doing less each year. Some advisors who have been in the business for a long time and are headed toward retirement will let their books decline at a certain point, so this wasn't a surprise. They start taking more time for themselves, so they're at work less and less, but their clients don't need them less. So when a client leaves, they don't have the availability to backfill the vacancy. In other words, they're not in client acquisition mode anymore, but in client maintenance mode, and the model for paring down the business has become attrition.

Toward the end of an advisor's career, they may be prone to lean toward the mentality of gliding through the process, sticking mainly to transactions, and maybe playing a little more golf. Jack had come to this point in his career several years *before* we met him. But he hadn't slacked off at all, thinking he could make his exit at the last minute. At the age of seventy-six he had still been proactive. He had gotten an idea of what his business was worth, talked to senior management about his options, and had even interviewed successful advisors in his office to see if one of them would be a good fit for taking over the business. Like I said, Jack had done everything right—almost.

In the middle of his vetting process, Jack's wife suffered from some medical issues, so he had to put his search on hold for a while, delaying his decision. When she was well enough, he picked it back up.

After spending some time mentoring one advisor in particular, Jack came to the conclusion that the person wasn't the right fit. Handing his business over to this person would be settling, and Jack wanted more for his clients and himself. By now, three years had passed.

So, when we met with Jack, he was in a different position than he had been when he'd started this journey. His timeline had shrunk, and because of his age and his wife's illness, his priorities had changed, too.

His outcome could have been catastrophic simply because he'd waited too long to begin planning for his next stage. Ideally, he would have started when he began his financial career, but we all know that rarely happens. Yet, he actually had a very good outcome. Our goal for Jack, like for all retiring financial advisors we work with, was to make him a hero on the way out and ourselves a hero on the way in. It was a win-win for everyone.

In joint appointments between Jack, his clients, and our team, we made sure it was clear that Jack's main concerns were always with the client. We began to take over some of the administrative tasks, allowing Jack time to start building his next chapter. We even threw him a retirement party and invited his best friends, neighbors, and clients to celebrate his life and career. Jack's family was grateful and he was humbled, because he could see that we appreciated everything he had done and he didn't have to worry whether or not we would continue to put the people he cared about first. Because we were such a great fit from a business, personality, and priorities perspective, the transition was easy. And even though Jack had a delayed start, he didn't have to forfeit his best next stage, a richer life, or time to keep making an impact in the world.

Jack's transition was pretty seamless. He was able to do introductions with our team, and we paired him with two advisors who best fit the client base. One was more localized in that market, working directly with the clients, while the other advisor spent more time with Jack as he transitioned out of the business. The deal structure allowed for Jack to be paid out 75 percent upfront with 25 percent on the back end, which was a terrific deal for an advisor in Jack's situation. It was a win for him financially, and it was a win for his clients. It was also a win for Jack's peace of mind. He doesn't feel like he has to come into the office or check in on his clients, and he's able to enjoy his next stage in life.

Jack did a lot of things right, but he had a bit of luck too, finding a firm that would work with him to ensure a great outcome. Imagine if he had started sooner, say in his 40s, 30s, or even at the start of his career. Imagine how planning for the next stage might have changed his life, his legacy, and his future when he had all the options and all the time to plan. Then again, imagine if he had started even later, like Tom did.

TOM

Tom was talking to multiple companies about setting up a continuity plan for succession. He wanted to know what they had to offer, but each time a buyer got down to the nitty-gritty, Tom pulled back. He wasn't mentally prepared to transition. After a number of fits and starts, he finally settled on the right company. He had a succession plan and a letter of intent in place, but he still wanted to ease into it, so none of it went into effect. He still wasn't ready to step away.

Slowly, he began moving his business and completing all the documentation. Several months into the process, the buyer noticed something in his conversations with Tom: he was having trouble communicating. He was literally forgetting words midsentence, financial terminology he'd been using every day for decades. The buyer asked Tom about it, and suggested he see his doctor for a checkup.

Tom did, and the news was devastating. He had a brain tumor. He immediately went into treatment, but he also moved forward with his succession. Tom wanted to spend time with his family, too, because he didn't know how much time he had left. The only fortunate piece of this is that he had begun the process, and so it could continue without him having to make a lot of decisions. The price had been negotiated, and the transition had started. He could have peace of mind, knowing his business and his clients were being taken care of, and his family would be taken care of financially. This freed him up to take care of himself.

Tom started late, but his situation could have been a lot worse. He might have not started to transition his business at all, and with his medical condition, transitioning his business could have been a disaster.

TOM'S STORY

Tom wasn't my client—he worked with Mark, an advisor at one of my sister companies. I spoke with Mark about Tom and want to share some of his insights here from that conversation.

Here's what Mark told me:

"When we think about what our business model is when it's at its best—when we're having the best impact that we can have—is often when somebody is going through a challenging situation. So we're constantly beating the drum that advisors should be focused on: developing a continuity plan for succession on their terms. Whether it can be implemented now, three to five years from now, or in the far future, we want them to have a catastrophic plan set up for worst-case scenarios.

"I was introduced to Tom, and we spent several months talking through a potential merger and how it would work, but he was really stuck on how to transition the business. He didn't know if he wanted to develop a succession plan or if he should stay affiliated for a while and just have a catastrophic plan on file. He was paralyzed in a way, unable to make a decision. He almost didn't make one, but we were able to help him understand that we would be flexible either way. This was really about him, and he needed to do some soul-searching with himself and his wife and his daughter. He had to identify what was most important to him, because we would be willing to implement any of those plans.

"About nine months later, Tom decided to move forward and transition the business. I think he and his wife were very excited to make that transition, because it was time for them to start enjoying themselves a bit more. The goal was to spend a couple months integrating our team and himself and clients together, and then Tom could take his first real winter off. He wanted to go to Florida and then come back in the spring to define his level of engagement. We were flexible, and open to that plan.

"Tom did go to Florida, but within a month, he was forgetting things—forgetting words, forgetting what we had discussed. I asked him to get checked out, and his doctor discovered a lesion on Tom's brain. He had brain cancer. Tom's situation is so tragic, but it could have been worse. He's had to spend his retirement battling for his life, but he isn't worried about what's happening with his business.

"I visited Tom recently at his home. He met me at the door and gave me a huge hug. 'I love that you're here,' he said, 'It's so great to see you. I love your team.'

"We spent a couple of hours just talking. He told me about his life, and what he was doing, and he talked a lot about his past. Then he said, 'I'm so glad we did what we did, and if I hadn't made the decision to do it, and I didn't have a plan, my wife would have been in a terrible position financially. My daughter would have likely been out of a job. My clients' things would have been in disarray. I'm so glad that I made this decision.

It's one less thing for me to worry about, so I can focus on spending time with my family and getting myself better.'

"On my drive back to my office, I was thinking about how good it felt to be able to provide flexibility and a multitude of options to people we work with so they can create the picture they want, and then execute it. Never had this belief resonated so strongly than when I thought of Tom, and how we were able to help him. It's one thing to see deals like this on paper, and another to see the impact on a person's life firsthand."

TAKING INVENTORY

Have you evaluated what your next stage in life looks like? Are you ready to start to take those next steps? If you are, understanding your options is critical. You don't want attrition to be your financial plan. You don't want your business to deplete over time, and for your clients to settle for less service because you want to take more time for yourself. You don't want your clients and your team to suffer if you or someone in your family has health problems, or any other type of emergency requiring your attention.

Take an inventory and take control. Answer all the questions that you may be avoiding. Don't settle for being one of the 73 percent of financial advisors who have no plan (no, I'm not kidding—73 percent). Start by taking inventory of your style of business—are you still operating in the Old World, or have you moved forward into the New World?

A Brave New World:
Take Inventory of Your Business Style

The Old World way of doing business was good, and it worked. If this is how you worked for your entire career, that's fine. But today, there is a brave New World way of doing business. Regulatory bodies prefer that we move to a service-based model, where transparency is the objective and serving clients and being a fiduciary is our duty.

I worked in the Old World model for many years, remember. I can still hear advisors making call after call, saying, "Mr. Jones, I think you should buy this stock or this bond," yet the advisor barely knew Mr. Jones. These days, to do your best for Mr. Jones, you have to know his life story. You have to know about his family, their challenges, and their goals. This business has shifted from an industry focused on sales to one focused on service, and to make this transition, you have to understand the people of today and how they're different from earlier generations.

A Changing Population:
Take Inventory of Diversity

Diversity is a major issue in our industry. Women account for fewer than 20 percent of the overall financial advisor demographic, and minorities make up an even smaller percentage. Yet your potential customer base is highly diverse. The average advisor in his 60s who has been in the business for thirty years may have many clients in their 70s and or 80s, but these are not the people who will account for the majority of your client base ten or twenty years from now. Evaluate the diversity in your book and see where the trend is heading. You are probably working with more younger people, more women, and more people of color than you were when you started. Is this same diversity reflected in your staff?

Look at your client base and look at their children, too, because more and more, you and whoever takes on your business will be working with a very different group of people. You may be meeting with mostly men because you started the relationship with them years ago, but today women make 87 percent of the buying decisions. Working only with the "man of the house" is Old World thinking, and it's as dated as running your business on a transactional model.

If women are becoming more involved in investing and are even better at it than men, they should be represented in your client book, and in your marketing material and advertising. Likewise, the Hispanic and African American populations are growing and gaining in wealth, yet their demographic, along with women, is underserved.

If you've been serving people within the same age range and of the same race and gender your whole career, think about adding people to your workforce who have worked with people of different age groups, races, and genders. And when you're looking at companies to consider for a merger, look at their staff. Are they looking at the current and future client investor market, or stuck in the past?

WOMEN, DOLLARS, AND SENSE

Whether you're a man or a woman, consider adding more women to your team. If you're used to talking to male clients, reach out to more women clients. It just makes sense.

Consider these stats from David Bach's bestseller, *Smart Women Finish Rich* (2016 edition):

- According to a 2016 Fidelity analysis of more than 8 million clients, women generated investment returns higher by 40 basis points, or about half a percent.
- According to a 1995 study by the National Association of Investors Corporation (now known as BetterInvesting.org), women's investment clubs outperformed men's clubs by 11 percent per year for 10 of the 12 years included in the study.
- The lifetime earning rate for women's investment groups was *significantly* better than for men—10.5 percent to 9.7 percent.
- According to the Boston Consulting Group, $39.6 trillion of the world's wealth is now controlled by women.
- Fidelity estimates that women now control 30 percent of global private wealth—up 25 percent in just five years—and it is estimated that women's wealth will grow by 7 percent annually.
- Women-owned businesses now employ nearly 9 million people and generate more than $1.7 trillion in revenue.
- According to the Bureau of Labor Statistics, there are now 73.5 million women in the US

workforce compared to just 18.4 million working women in 1950. This is leading to record levels of wealth for women.

- The percentage of women who have at least $1 million in their 401(k) accounts has doubled in the past decade, climbing from 10 percent of female 401(k) holders in 2005 to 20 percent as of 2017, according to Fidelity.
- According to the American College of Financial Services, women make up 45 percent of all American millionaires.[9]

DIVERSITY BY THE NUMBERS

Charts such as those on the website wealthmanagement.com illustrate the lack of diversity in the financial services market. Their data shows the following:

- The total value of assets under management, the global AUM, was $71.4 trillion in 2015.
- Assets managed by firms owned by women or minorities was just 1.1 percent of that amount.
- That means 98.9 percent of assets are managed by firms owned by white males. (Fact. No hate.../ am one.)
- Asset management is among the least diverse industries in America.
- Within the US population, 63 percent are Caucasian, 36 percent are Hispanic, 12.2 percent are African American, and 5.6 percent are Asian.

---

9   David Bach, *Smart Women Finish Rich, Expanded and Updated* (New York: Currency, 2018).

- Yet among financial advisors, 79 percent are white, 7.1 percent are Hispanic or Latino, 8.1 percent are African American, and 5.7 percent are Asian.
- There are 434,000 financial advisors in the US.
- Mutual funds: Total AUM for mutual funds is 47 trillion. 0.9 percent are AUM managed by women-owned firms, which is 4.23 billion. And 0.3 percent are minority-owned firms, 1.41 billion. Regarding the ratio profile for financial advisors, this is probably one that looks better to use: 81 percent are white, 7 percent are Asian, 6 percent are African American, 5 percent are Hispanic, and 1 percent other.
- A 2018 article by MarketWatch references that only 16 percent of all financial advisors, roughly 49,000, are women.

In addition to gender, age, and race diversity, your clients have different lifestyles and living situations. You may have same-sex couples, unmarried couples with children, couples whose parents live with them, and couples whose adult children share their home.

One of my clients came to me after working with another firm that his parents had recommended. The client said that after contacting this advisor, he received a manila envelope in the mail filled with a packet of thirty pages of forms for him to fill out. The advisory firm wanted him to set up a bunch of appointments. The man was thirty years old and was astonished that anyone would think for a minute that he would do this.

He told me, "I wanted to fill out a five-minute online questionnaire, have them tell me what to bring in, and then have one face-to-face appointment on a video conference like GoToMeeting or Zoom." The client thought that having someone come to his house was archaic. He, and many people like him, do all their business online, and they expect their advisors to be current with technology.

Rembrandts in the Attic:
Take Inventory of Your Hidden Gems

When you're taking inventory of your business, don't overlook your Rembrandts in the attic, a concept I learned about from John Ratliff speaking on stage about selling businesses at Joe Polish's *Genius Network*,[10] a networking group for forward-thinking entrepreneurs. Think of it like this: Would you pay more for a home if you knew there was a Rembrandt, a Picasso, or a Dali hidden in the attic? These are the assets that make your business special: processes you've developed that work really well, tribal knowledge you've developed and documented, and any other items of value that you may take for granted, but add value to your business.

You may have Rembrandts among your clients, too. Over the years, if you've gotten lax about prospecting and really deep-diving your book of business, you may have clients who would do a lot more with you if you asked. If

---

10 "THE $65 MILLION SECRET: How To Build A Business That Is Worth Selling (Even If You Never Do)," *Genius Network*, https://geniusnetwork.com/65millionsecret/.

you actively seek out the Rembrandts, you'll find money in transition you didn't even know was out there, that your clients just sit on because they don't know what else to do with it. When I take on a mature book, I almost always find money. But first I have to get to know the client. I look at what their current advisor thinks they have, but I make no assumptions that it's the totality of their investment potential. So much is missed over the years, and unless you ask, your clients will typically not ask you what they should do with it. Questions that uncover Rembrandts should be part of any company's checklist when they acquire or merge with another business, but if you do it beforehand, your business will have more value to them.

Take Inventory of Your Client Relationship Management

Even the way you contact your clients could be your Rembrandt in the attic, especially if it's organized and effective. This could exist in your third-party CRM, or it may be a proprietary system developed by your team. My team developed the cycle that we call the Freedom Street Contact Management System, which meets our clients' needs and is extremely scalable, so we can add new clients seamlessly. The cycle is based on the calendar year.

In January, our calls focus on income needs. This is a simple fifteen-minute phone call where we tackle things like RMDs, income needs for the year, upcoming big purchases, etc.

In February, we host a town hall for clients and their friends, and we provide a market update. For those who don't wish to attend in person, we hold a second town hall via teleconference.

March and April are referred to as "flex time" because people are doing their taxes and they have reactive needs. Instead of proactive calling, we make ourselves available to answer their questions and are usually more proactive with the clients' CPAs. Our high-net-worth clients will need a bit more attention as well.

In May, we focus on our client's risk assessments, and in June, we invite everyone out for a big multi-generational family-style summer barbecue.

July and August are more flex time, because people are on vacation and spending more time with their families, so it's difficult to connect with them sometimes. Here's a good chance for us to focus on practice management and planning.

We start another call cycle in September, and these calls focus on performance. We talk about where clients are versus where they want to be and discuss whether they should be making any changes to their strategy.

December is when we invite clients and their families to join us for a large, open house party.

This is my system, and it works for my clients in my market. Yours may be different, so you need to look at whom you are serving and what would work best for them.

ARE YOU REPLACEABLE?

Companies looking to work with you as you transition out of your business want to see that you've established great relationships with your clients. They also want to know that you're the prophet and not the god. If you're the only person clients can rely on, your business might be less scalable and less sellable than you think.

Other companies will want to see an engaged staff, so make sure that your team is involved with your clients and not just making appointments and answering the phone. The more your team is involved, the easier it will be for the new company to repeat what your company is doing without you being that sole contact for clients.

If you're looking to sell, continue to maintain those strong relationships, but be realistic about another team taking over, and how much sense it makes for them to meet every one of your clients in person every quarter. Most likely, they can manage the relationships and the portfolios with an established number of face-to-face meetings a year. Different clients require different levels of contact. If you have a large client base and you're meeting with every person four times a year, another company won't be able to manage the workload. If you have a smaller base of only high-net-worth clients, they will, and your business will be more attractive to them. Supplement your meetings with regular email, phone, and mail touches over the course of the year. Birthday and holiday cards are another way to reach out to clients to let them know you're thinking of them, without burdening yourself and your staff with more appointments than are really necessary, and that your clients don't want or need. A system of touches like this is repeatable, and another company can easily duplicate it.

If you're worried that your clients will be let down if you aren't constantly calling on them for appointments, consider how much has changed since you became an advisor. People have gotten used to email, phone, and Zoom; they don't demand or even expect as much in-person face time as they used to. A young advisor I know put it like this: "My clients don't want to hear from me all the time. They want less contact, but they want quality contact. I proactively reach out to them and I answer their questions, but we only need one appointment a year. We set a course and stick to it. Unless there's a major change in their situation, we don't need another sit-down." Basically, as you get to know your clients, you should get a feel for how much attention they want and need. You don't want them so dependent on you and alarmed every time there's a blip in the market, but you also want them to know you're there when they need you. It's a happy balance that your clients appreciate and that you can maintain and hand off to another advisory team. Remember, this is *one* example of an advisor in a major city and fast-paced environment. Where your clients live matters, and the demographics of your area can make a big difference in their expectations. You know better than anyone how much face-to-face time people need.

That predictability and sustainability with your relationships should also be reflected in how you run your business. More revenue, more assets, and more clients are not always the recipe for a successful continuity plan or succession. The key is to make the revenue predictable, and to make sure that there are recurring revenue sources. This requires a service model for your clients that's based on a contract and investment policy statement. People are willing to pay a premium for predictable cash flow, and predictable cash flow comes from recurring revenue.

WHO'S YOUR AUDIENCE?

Segmenting your client base helps you reach out to those who need more touches and leave the people alone who don't like that much communication. But it's not always clear cut.

For example, when the market's not doing well and I email my clients an explanation of what's going on, I tend to hear from people who aren't used to email communication. My older clients see it as an alarm, and they call to ask me if they should be worried. The younger clients, on the other hand, are used to knowing what's going on all the time—they grew up on the internet. So they read the email—or not—and go on with their lives.

QUESTIONS TO ASK YOURSELF

Before you start vetting companies, vet yourself. The questions you ask yourself are similar to those you'd ask clients when you create a financial plan.

1. What is my current situation?
2. Who are my clients?

3. How movable is my book of business?

4. What is the value of my business today?

5. What is the age demographic of my total business right now?

6. How many assets and accounts are multigenerational?

7. How do I want to step away from the business?

8. What is my niche and what types of clients do I service?

9. Are there other advisors in my area or demographic that specialize in my niche and client type?

10. Should I be looking for advisors who specialize in succession and transition and catastrophic risk?

11. Have I segmented my book of business and identified those clients who need more of my attention and those who prefer less contact?

12. Should my first step be affiliating/merging with another company?

13. Do I need to create a true continuity plan, a succession plan?

14. What is the plan, and who is going to execute it?

15. What is the price point at which it would be executed?

16. What's the value of my practice? Be realistic.

17. Does it make more sense to sell the business outright?

EVERY ADVISOR'S INVENTORY— AND BEST NEXT STEP—IS DIFFERENT

Your situation probably isn't identical to Jack's or Tom's or any other advisor's. No two people in this business are dealing with the exact same circumstances. Your inventory is different than mine; your client base is different than mine. You have processes that are—or could be—repeatable and scalable. You're a prophet, a god, or somewhere between in your business. You have your own niche and your own Rembrandts, and they probably look very different than what I have in my attic. I know advisors who work solely with doctors, lawyers, or engineers. Some take on only high-net-worth clients, while others work with clients from one specific corporation. Your clients and inventories are unique to you and are a big part of what makes your business different.

But in my years of working with advisors, I've noticed many similarities that advisors share around their goals, strengths, and challenges, typically—although not always—tied to how long they've been in the business. My advice for seasoned, midpoint, and rookie advisors can apply to people at any stage.

Seasoned Advisor

The seasoned advisor typically has twenty years or longer in the business. He's enjoyed upturns and survived downturns and has had a certain amount of success. He has a good staff and solid processes in place.

The Seasoned Advisor's Concerns

The seasoned advisor is—at the very least—thinking about a continuity plan. Should he be looking at a merger or a succession? He's worried about what would become of his business and his family if something happened to him. This guy probably isn't ready to retire, but he's looking ahead and thinking that someday he might want to.

What will that look like? How will it play out? The seasoned advisor is worried about how his next stage will affect his family at home. He's also concerned for his work family. He knows they're counting on him for their income, and they have families at home too. This advisor knows that some of his staff is stellar and if he chooses to sell his firm, they'll be considered valuable assets. He also has a few people on his team who aren't doing well and will likely not survive a sale or merger.

What the Seasoned Advisor Can Do Right Now

A seasoned advisor needs to know what their practice is worth. He should not only have a valuation, but also evaluate internal systems. Are they streamlined? Repeatable? Do most tasks rely on the advisor being involved, or are there activities that his staff handles on a regular basis? What about when he goes on vacation? Is there someone in place to cover for him?

This advisor should look beyond just having a good staff to having a *diverse* staff. At one time, his staff may have reflected the marketplace, but times and the marketplace have changed. His existing client base may be getting older, but his new clients are younger. They're racially diverse, and there are a lot of women looking for a great advisor. Does his business reflect this growing market? Does his staff understand the needs of this diverse customer base? Are we delivering service based on what our business *was*, or who it is *now*?

The Midpoint Advisor

The financial advisor who's been in the business for ten to twenty years is still in acquisition mode. She's building her business, bringing on staff, and starting to create processes. She hasn't had to deal with many (or any) downturns and has been enjoying steady success for most of her career.

The Midpoint Advisor's Concerns

The midpoint advisor is thinking about where she is right now and where she wants to be for the rest of her career. She might have $100 million under management and striving for $200 million. This advisor looks at her career as a sort of marriage, thinking *I got married young and for all the right reasons, but are we growing together or apart?*

The midpoint advisor is past the difficult years of trying to make it and is looking at her current base, the foundational structure she's in, and the people with whom she's aligned herself. She could be an employee at a firm yet have an entrepreneurial spirit that isn't a good fit at her firm.

Maybe she has great ideas that are always being rejected. Or she might want to do more social media but her firm doesn't allow it. This advisor may also be running her own business and feeling that she'd rather move her business to a big firm.

What the Midpoint Advisor Can Do Right Now
Like the seasoned advisor, the midpoint advisor should also be evaluating where she stands. I was at the midpoint of my career—less than fifteen years in—when I began evaluating my identity and moved from the employee model to become an independent advisor. My recommendation is to take a step back every five years and look at where you are, and how it aligns with the person you want to be and the kind of business you want to be associated with. A lot can change in five years, and you, yourself, can change a lot. What felt like the right choice for you five years ago may be way off the mark for what you want your career to look like today, or five years from now.

If this is you, consider if you're with the right firm. Is it a good fit? Is it servicing your ideal client base or niche? Do you connect with your team or is it time to move on? This is the time to think about your choices. If you don't, you'll continue on the same path for years, when you could be on a path that takes better advantage of your passions and your skills and is more fulfilling to you professionally and personally.

If you've been with a company for a certain amount of time, comfort sets in, along with a fear of change. This fear makes it hard to leave, even to move on to something better. But true wealth—and true happiness—comes from the stupid decisions that you didn't make, not the decisions that you did. The definitive decisions that we make are usually good ones. But it's the ones you don't even think about and neglect to make, like moving to another firm that might fit you better, that can cost you big in the future.

Time goes by fast, and the longer you're in the business, the faster it flies. Don't wait until you're ready to retire to look back on your career and think, *What could I have done different or better?* Ask yourself those questions now and throughout your career, and you will create major moments in minor times.

The Rookie Advisor

This advisor has less than ten years of experience. He's part of a team and still establishing himself in the business.

The Rookie Advisor's Concerns

This early in his career, the advisor is learning the ropes and just trying to survive. He feels like there's so much to learn, and he's evaluating what designations are going to matter to him. The rookie is usually working side by side with another advisor in a mentorship arrangement. He's going through the motions, hopeful that he'll be successful, and he wakes up every day wishing he were further along in his career. The rookie wants his clients to succeed, and he wants to do everything right the first time to build a firm foundation for his business.

What the Rookie Advisor Can Do Right Now

You might think that taking inventory isn't important at this stage. But the truth is, the rookie advisor tends to get caught up in a lot of activity and neglects to see how the future will play out. If he can start thinking about what he wants the end to look like now, he can guide himself along a more direct path to get there.

If this is you, think about the types of clients you want to service. Zero in on them and figure out how best to work with them. Find a practice to tap into that reflects the kind of service model you need, and let others tend to the daily minutiae so you can focus on client relationships. That's what will provide true value to the future of your practice.

This is a great time to find your niche. Increase your designations and figure out where you fit. Then position yourself throughout the coming years to methodically build value with a goal in mind.

Just like advisors who have been in the business for a while, you should look around at whom you're working with and whom you service. Is your market diverse? What about your team? What is that market going to be in ten or twenty years, and how will that team meet their needs?

KNOW YOUR INVENTORY

Taking an inventory requires you to look at your practice from many angles. Look at where you are now and where your business will be based on the trajectory. Look at the demographics and the diversity within your company. I'm not suggesting you hire anyone specifically based on their race or gender. But identify the age demographic and the diversity of your practice and ask yourself if your clients' needs are being met. Then hire the best *human* for the job (that's my motto!).

HIRE THE BEST HUMAN—
BUT DON'T IGNORE THESE FACTS

The US Census Bureau of 2016 shows that women make up 49–51 percent of the country's population. The Bureau of Labor Statistics states that women account for 35.5 percent of financial advisors. However, when you include the heads of brokerage, that number shrinks to just 14 percent. Perhaps even more important is this: **55 percent of women between twenty-five and thirty-four prefer working with female financial advisors, and 70 percent of women will leave their advisor within a year when they become widowed.**

By taking inventory and auditing your practice, you will be better prepared to pivot when you need to pivot. Whether that is to merge, acquire, sell, or to have a succession plan in place, knowing where you stand lets you do your fiduciary duty and have a continuity plan for your clients. Prepare and have a plan so that when you want to or have to separate, you can, on your timeline.

CHAPTER SEVEN QUESTIONS

1. What stage are you in?

2. Is your practice where you want it to be?

3. Are your people in the right roles?

4. Is your team complete or incomplete?

CHAPTER 8

Your Exit Strategy and Next Stage

The heaviness of being successful was replaced by the lightness of being a beginner again, less sure about everything. It freed me to enter one of the most creative periods of my life.
—Steve Jobs

No matter where you are in your business, you can change it. You might be drowning in paperwork, regulations, and chaos, but over time, you can fix whatever's broken.

I told you about Hardworking Hank in chapter 1, the guy whose business was running him. After I got to know Hank, two things became clear: he wanted our help, and we wanted to help him. I flew out to visit his offices and see what we were dealing with.

Hank was working out of a tiny office in an older part of town. The reception area was dark with wood paneling and wall-to-wall filing cabinets. His office was crowded and his desk overflowed with paperwork. I pulled up a chair and started asking Hank some basic questions.

"Tell me about your process."

"I don't really have a process," he said.

"What about your systems? What do you do about risk?" He didn't have a system for risk. He didn't have an online filing system either, or a system for managing compliance. To be fair, Hank knew all about his clients. If I asked him to tell me about Mr. Johnson, he could relate every detail of the client's financial situation to me, along with lots of personal information. He knew his clients intimately and could recite all their stories. Hank was a great advisor. But he was doing things the old-fashioned way, and it was sucking the life out of him.

I was extremely confident that Hank had all the tools to be successful; so to start, I initiated a coaching relationship with him. Under the guidance of our team, I believed Hank could grow his business exponentially in a short time.

We met with Hank several times and worked with him long-distance on a daily basis. He used my staff and we showed him how to streamline his work and hand much of it off to an assistant. Then we had him revisit every client. He reevaluated every client's risk and set up an investment policy statement for each one with tools that we shared with him and showed him how to use. Hank also started talking to each client about his business model and how he now had more to offer them, thanks to the innovative methods he had access to, working with our team. He did this one conversation at a time and showed them how it would change the way he managed not only their portfolios, but also their financial lives.

One year later, Hank had turned his practice around. Through our systems and processes, he started to execute on our investment management best practices. Hank was utilizing our marketing and branding, offering client events, and leveraging our client relationship management system. His new level of confidence carried over to his clients, whose confidence in Hank grew along with his business. In addition to his part-time receptionist, he brought on full-time staff to make the most of the new systems. Working with my team was a catalyst for big changes in Hank's professional and personal life.

Suddenly, he had even more time to attend his kids' soccer games. He had time to take them to professional basketball games. He took a long weekend and went to Las Vegas with his girlfriend. Finally, Hank could go away for a few days and not worry about things falling apart. His life changed completely, and he looked forward to going into the office and seeing his clients. He exuded positivity and a can-do attitude, and all those old, overwhelming concerns about cash, clients, compliance, and the next chapter of his career went away.

Fast-forward a few years and Hank crossed over $1 million a year in production. His business's valuation nearly quadrupled. He built a brand-new office in the town square—the first new building the area had seen in more than forty years. I went to the grand opening and ribbon-cutting, and hundreds of people from the community showed up. I could see the pride on Hank's face and on the faces of those people, and that pride was contagious.

Standing beside my friend and colleague was a humbling experience for me, and an honor. It was clear that Hank was making an impact in his community and living a legacy that would survive for years—maybe generations.

Hank's still at it, and his business is still growing. Reenergized, Hank has taken back his business and his life, and he owns his future. He wants to keep working, but when the time comes, he will be ready for it. He has a full continuity plan, and whether he needs it for a catastrophe or succession, he's prepared.

Even though it was a changing regulatory environment that spurred Hank to ask for help, getting his compliance in order was just one of a multitude of benefits he enjoyed in the short time he worked with us. And now his business is positioned to deliver him to his next chapter, whatever he wants that to be.

YOUR NEXT STAGE

Again, no matter where you are in your business, you can turn it around. And by now, you have a good idea of where you are and where you want to be. The next step is defining exactly what the next stage looks like. Then you can create a plan to get there, and finally, execute on it.

I was in a dinner meeting with a $3 million producer who's crushing it in a very specific niche. He has a good team and good systems, but he's plateaued. He's okay with that, because honestly, he's in a pretty good place. Our conversation turned to catastrophic risk plans and succession plans, and it was obvious that this advisor didn't have either in place, and no plans to make them, because he was happy to keep doing what he was doing. His wife, who's the operations manager, was in the meeting and she said to him, "We're doing amazing, but it's time to either replicate what we're doing so we can scale, or we need to get out. I love and respect what we've done, but I feel it's time for us to move on. I have other goals in my life."

This woman knew there was more to life than what she was doing, and it was time for her to do it. Not everyone thinks that way, though; not because they don't have goals, but because they've never even considered the fact that other goals were possible. When you're having that level of success, you tend to believe that staying on track is the best course.

If I told you that what you're doing right now is exactly what you're going to be doing for the next ten years, would you stay, or step away? Do you love every facet of your job so much that you can see yourself doing it every day for the next decade?

Most likely, there is something about your job that you really enjoy. What if you could spend the next ten years building out those parts of your career, and letting go of the parts you don't enjoy? How might that change your life?

These questions took our conversation in a new direction. The advisor told me he was, what he referred to as, "wasting" $700,000 a year on firm admin fees necessary to support his production. What he really loved most about his work, though—what lit him up—was the marketing, speaking engagements, and presentations. So we talked about what he could do if he diverted $100,000 of what he paid for unnecessary admin fees toward marketing his niche.

I took it a step further: "Imagine if you applied $45,000 towards building out a book on the processes in your niche, and another $35,000 to $40,000 on videos and webinars for teaching that niche. And a few more thousand on a platform for replicating it for other advisors, where you can train them to do what you're doing, so they can serve even more clients the way you're serving them? Now, what if you took that entire $700,000 and applied it toward that. How much would you be producing then?"

He admitted that he had never thought about it, but it was a dream scenario: doing what he loves and what he's best at and making a lot more money doing it.

We spent the rest of the dinner talking about a catastrophic risk plan and a succession plan, which he needed, with the understanding that he first needed a foundation built on what would really make him and his wife happy. There is no sense in continuing to grow a business that you don't love, no matter how many millions you're producing. To get there, we had to stop focusing on the money and focus on what, ultimately, would make these two people so happy that they could see themselves doing it for the next decade or longer.

YOU'RE AN ADVISOR—
DO YOU REALLY NEED A PLAN?

Let's get serious for a minute about why a succession plan is necessary. If something happened to you tomorrow, what would happen to your business and how would that affect your family? What would be the impact to your associates, employees, and clients?

If your practice were sold to an internal party, would they pay the full value? How much of a difference would it be from the going rate in today's market? Or would an external buyer be willing to pay much more? With no plan in place, how much control would you have over that transition in the event of a catastrophic event?

Who would take care of your clients and the multigenerational families you've guided through all their financial matters? Would they be divided up among rookie advisors with little or no experience? Do you have a continuity plan for your clients, and don't they deserve one?

These are some of the questions I ask advisors, and while they all agree they need to have a plan, few are willing to actually develop one. They're not ready for the next stage, and I get that, but it's kind of like hide and seek—ready or not, it's coming. I don't expect anyone to just throw up their hands and say, "Okay, it's over!" I do want them to visualize what the next stage looks like and then take a couple of steps to prepare for it.

High producers especially don't want to think about it. For a basic example, if you're doing $3 million a year in revenue, and you're looking at selling your practice for full value—maybe two and a half times revenue—that might get you $7.5 million. This is like getting a $7.5 million advance but giving up all future earnings. Without that consistent cash flow, how will you maintain your current lifestyle?

That's hard to think about, but you have to think about it in order to start planning for the next stage. This doesn't mean you are going to sell your business next year—only that when the time comes, you will be prepared to sell it for its full value, and not leave your family, your team, and your clients high and dry.

In an earlier chapter, we talked about your Rembrandts in the attic. You may have Rembrandts among your staff who are indispensable. In some offices, there is an assistant, an administrator, an operations manager, or executive secretary who holds the place together. Some of these people speak with clients more than the advisor does. While you should speak with all of your staff about the next stage for your business, these people in particular need to be part of that conversation. If you left, would they want to keep working at your firm? Don't assume they would want to stay or go. Ask.

Everyone knows they need a plan, and most people want to know the steps to create one. But few people first take the time to examine what the end result of that plan will look like for all involved, or to ask everyone affected what they see as the ideal outcome. It's your job, as the advisor, to ask them.

TRANSITION STATISTICS

A 2018 study by FP Transitions, LLC, discovered the following regarding financial advisor acquisitions:

There are approximately eighty-five inquiries for every one seller.

The average business stays on the market for twenty-eight weeks.

The average transaction is $2.4 million.

In an acquisition, the average seller is sixty-one years old.

In a merger, the average age is fifty-six.[11]

EVALUATE YOUR OPTIONS

Your next stage can be whatever you want it to be, but generally speaking, you have three options for moving away from your current position in the business: acquisition, which is selling your business; affiliation, which entails merging or aligning with another organization; and succession, where you merge and eventually exit on a set date in the future.

---

11   FP Transitions, "M&A Report: Trends in Transactions and Valuation Study," 2019.

Selling

This option is for the advisor who wants to step down quickly. If you've decided to retire or move on to another career, an acquisition is going to be the fastest exit strategy. The average age of advisors who choose this route is sixty-one, and it's been climbing over the years.

Why Selling Makes Sense

More financing options are available today, which means more offers to buy your business. Beyond owner financing, the bigger banks are getting in on the action.

The bottom line is there are a lot of reasons to separate from a business, and many of them stem from a place of urgency. Maybe the market is good, and there's a lot of interest in your firm. You can sell quickly at a great price. Or maybe your health is suffering and you want to stop working, or your spouse is getting up in years and you want to spend more time together. All these reasons can pressure you to sell without doing your due diligence. It's tempting to avoid the minutia and make a fast, clean break. The money can be exciting, but you have to remember that this is really about your clients and your future.

Another reason advisors sometimes sell too quickly is to avoid a down market. When the markets are doing well and potentially at an all-time high, they want to get out before there's any more volatility to deal with. If they're right, separating now maximizes their investment. Are they wrong to think that way? Still other advisors simply want to move on to another career. They may have been in the business for twenty years and want to monetize now. Then they can move on to their next chapter, whatever that is.

These can all be valid reasons for choosing acquisition. But no matter how attractive selling your business appears, rushing into it without considering what happens next for you and for your clients can lead to less-than-ideal consequences.

Why You Shouldn't Rush an Acquisition
Earlier, I told you about Jack and how he had transitioned out of his business. Working with advisors like Jack and speaking with many other advisors about their transition experiences, I've learned a lot about what can go wrong and how to avoid it. The challenges aren't obvious, and when you're hot to sell your business and getting offers from everywhere, it's tempting to move full steam ahead. But you have to take your time. This is a big deal that will affect you, your clients, your family, and your "work family" for years.

What to Ask When You're Selling
If you decide to sell to an advisor, make sure they can actually do the deal. You might get eighty initial inquiries, with about fifty of those being serious buyers. Those who actually qualify are a small percentage of that group.

Beyond the finances, you need to coordinate with the buyer on a lot of things so you understand the direction they plan to take your business. A buyer with the money isn't always a buyer with good processes. Be prepared to ask them how the transition will affect everyone involved:

- What is the experience going to be for my clients?

- What is the experience going to be for me?

- Is there a claw back? How are you protected? You can't just sell your book and expect to be done with all of it immediately—you need to transition your clients.

- What steps will you take to ensure clients remain with the business after you're gone?

- Will my current team stay on with the business?

When I work with an advisor who's selling their business, I discuss our investment strategy. I tell them how my team treats clients, and I explain our client relationship management strategy. I want the advisor to know how we interact with clients on a day-to-day basis. These important discussions should not be overlooked or taken for granted. Your idea of great service, after all, could be very different from another advisor's. You have to get the details: What is the business's infrastructure? Adding a business to their own creates exponential growth; how will they handle the new activity? Do they plan to expand their staff to accommodate your clients?

Thinking Ahead

Being acquired doesn't mean you're abandoning your clients, though. You have to think through how this will affect them. You also have to consider how it affects your family at home, and your work family.

Don't Abandon Your Skills in an Acquisition

When I've worked with businesses on an acquisition, too often the first question I get is, "What are you offering?" They want to hook up, and we haven't even been on a first date. I ask them to take a step back and pretend I'm a new client. What's their first step?

They know the answer to that question: "We want to get to know you and understand your goals and objectives."

Guess what? It's the same deal. Do you really want to sell your business to another advisor without understanding their intentions? What are their plans for this business that you've devoted years of your life to? Wouldn't you want to know *that*?

When I look at acquiring a business, I first need to understand the seller's needs, objectives, and timeline. I want to know about their book of business and their client base, including some of the finer details of that client base. Once I know the seller and the business, I understand what we're solving for and can structure the deal to fit.

Unlike a merger, an acquisition typically has a shorter timeline. The buyer needs to have a lot of information upfront, and having a valuation done ahead of time is helpful to all parties involved. Both the buyer and the seller should have a realistic expectation of the firm's value before entering into any serious talks about a deal.

Affiliation

When you don't want to step down right away, but you want to make a move that allows you to do so in time, your best option could be an affiliation. Affiliations and partnerships are like mergers. They allow you to become a part of something bigger than yourself with like-minded individuals. At the same time, this team approach protects your business with a catastrophic risk plan and gives you a platform and a plan for an eventual succession from the business.

When I welcome independent advisors to merge with my practice, they maintain their independence while reaping the benefits of being part of a bigger firm with its shared services model and other assets. This is often referred to as a "plug-and-play" model because the advisor plugs their business into the highly efficient and effective systems already in place in ours. However the advisor affiliates with us, there is always a continuity plan and an increased likelihood for a happy ending.

Succession

A succession plan can extend for three, five, ten years or longer, taking an advisor from today to whenever they're ready to begin their next chapter. That's why I love succession plans—they allow you to ease into them because they're not immediate. The plan could have no data at all, and many don't, especially at first. What a succession plan does is put someone you trust in place who's prepared to take over your practice and support your clients when you are ready to step away.

I've seen advisors try to create a succession by training a junior advisor. But taking a person who is new to the business from A to Z is difficult and may take years. Advisors may also want to hand off the business to their son or daughter, yet they have unrealistic expectations. Whether we're too hard or too soft on our children in the business, unless they know the ropes, it's going to be a difficult transition.

It can make more sense, in this situation, to opt for an acquisition or affiliation, working closely with the new firm to ensure your son or daughter is involved and will be properly trained and developed within the new firm, as a new advisor would be. In my experience, a son or daughter who can take over a business and hit the ground running is the exception. These are just a few of the many potential considerations that affect how you structure the deal, whether it's an acquisition, affiliation, or a succession.

SUCCESSION, ACQUISITION, OR AFFILIATION?

SUCCESSION: According to the Financial Planning Association, 73 percent of advisors do not have a written succession plan. Are you like the majority of advisors who are not certain who, when, and how you are going to transition your business? It's important to define when and how you want to slow down and transition responsibilities to another team, whether it is as simple as a catastrophic buy/sell agreement or a formal continuity plan. This will create peace of mind for you, your family, your clients, and your employees.

ACQUISITION: Many advisors are ready to take a significant step back, but they are still looking for the right successor. Whether you are looking to fully retire or want to remain engaged in some capacity, it's important to find experience, a customized approach, and strong financials that will allow you to sell your business on your terms. Each deal should be uniquely customized to the specific needs and goals of you and your team.

AFFILIATION: It is no surprise that more advisors are considering going independent than ever before. Unfortunately, many of them have yet to move because of the many complexities of operating a business from managing compliance and legal requirements to hiring and managing employees. Whether you are looking for the blueprint to building an independent practice or want to outsource components of operating your business, there are platforms that have the tools and resources you need to continue to own and operate your business.

WHAT TO DO IN THE SHORT TERM

While you're thinking over your options, there are plenty of actions you should take right now. Regardless of your situation or your timeline, you'll need to tackle these at some point. My list of recommended reading at the end of this book will help you define what to do without getting lost in the weeds.

Get a Valuation

If you haven't had a valuation in the last three years, schedule one. You need to know what your business is worth so you can establish a goal for next year, five years from now, and for whenever you decide to exit the business. Some companies work with banks to certify financial firms for funding so that when you want to sell your business, the buyer knows that what you say about its worth is accurate. These companies can do a valuation for you at any time for a fee.

I recommend getting a valuation a *minimum* of once every five years because your business changes so much in that time, and the valuation will change. If it doesn't, then you need to figure out why. You should be growing and not losing business, thriving and not dying. A valuation will tell you where you stand.

Make and Follow an Exit Strategy Checklist

Two to four years prior to exiting your business, start working your way through this checklist:

1. Identify your exit needs and goals.

2. Assemble a succession support team.

3. Get a preliminary business valuation.

4. Find a succession consultant.

5. If you're look at having a succession, review your continuity plan. Understanding the documentation is extremely important, including the letter of intent, asset sale agreement, consulting agreement, promissory notes, security guarantees, and any other agreements that exist.

6. Do your due diligence to prepare reports and documentation that cover the following:

   a. Client demographics
   b. Revenue history
   c. Key business systems that are important for the transition
   d. Asset demographics
   e. Processes

7. Identify your business value drivers.

8. Prepare your books, records, and accounting.

9. Update client files with as much detail as possible.

10. Understand CRM system compatibility.

11. Determine ideal successor profiles. Who's the right mate?

12. Visualize success—identify ideal exit goals.

13. Layout action steps to meet those exit goals.

14. On the client relationship side, make sure you've strengthened your client relationships.

One year prior to succession, focus on the following:

1. As you get closer to a succession, get to know the advisor who will be taking over.

2. Communicate with your key employees so they understand the timeline.

3. Obtain a certified valuation that can be used with banks.

4. Update a continuity partner to a successor.

5. Hire the right team for the transition:

a. A transition coach
b. An attorney
c. A tax specialist
d. A business broker
e. A valuation expert

6. Establish bank relationships, a letter of intent, and confidentiality agreements. It's very important to have confidentiality agreements because you're sharing the internal documents and internal structure of your practice with potential acquirers. You have to allow for due diligence inquiries of potential acquirers with current data.

7. Review the demographics of age and client assets, revenue history, and the systems that exist for transition.

8. Prepare client lists. Segment those lists for communication and meetings, and go to market, and then client relationships.

Three to six months before succession, do the following:

1. Complete negotiations.

2. If allowable, begin informing key clients of your intention to retire.

3. Begin introducing your key clients to the idea of your exit, and if a successor is chosen, describe the process.

4. Provide instructions and agreements to your broker-dealer.

5. Finalize all the documents listed above plus the following: asset sale agreement, consulting agreement, promissory notes, security guarantees, client communications pieces, account updates, or re-papering needs, and instructions to broker-dealer.

6. Have your trusted specialists—including your lawyer, tax specialist, and broker—make sure you have done your due diligence regarding all documentation, and everything is there.

7. Make sure your staff knows what's happening, and exactly what the timeline looks like.

8. Verify reassignment process with any of the key partners and the broker-dealer.

9. Prepare all client communication pieces and communication scheduling.

10. Make decisions regarding the roles and responsibilities of all parties existing.

11. Keep the clients in the loop.

12. Introduce the successor, and make sure that they're getting one-on-one meetings and you're face-to-facing with clients, introducing them in a way where you exit a hero and they enter a hero.

On the closing date, you have more to do:

1. Deliver on the terms.

2. Begin communication.

3. Re-paper, if needed, any documentation.

4. Sign all documents.

5. Start client communication.

6. Send the letters of instruction to the broker-dealer.

7. Communicate with staff, and then send all the client communication.

Finally, there is the process of post-closing:

1. Track all the accounts.

2. Focus on client transition, and provide transition support if applicable.

3. Continue consulting if needed.

4. While you're enjoying your retirement, you will still need to track account reassignment, the broker-dealer key business partners, and revenue transition per all your agreements to make sure you're meeting them.

The key to the success of your transition relies on the transfer of your client relationships. Following a client meeting schedule, re-paper where necessary as you phase out over a six- to twelve-month period.

You may be doing this yourself, but if you're merging with a company that specializes in taking on new businesses, they will do a lot of the work and step you through whatever they need from you. An acquiring company will typically guide you in this process from start to finish, working with you through your succession, acquisition, or affiliation, rather than expect you to do it on your own.

Revisit Your Personality Assessments

If you haven't already taken a personality assessment, this is a good time to do it. Understanding your personality strengths and how you interact with people always matters in our industry and is especially important when you start to step away. If you are a hard-charging, results-oriented individual, and you gear up with another hard-charging results-driven individual, the process may be very difficult for you.

Revisit the personality assessments of your team too. Identify who on your team is going to work well with those on the new team, so there's a balance of strengths and blind spots. How each person communicates and sees the world, and what's most important to them when it comes to processing that information, is different for everyone. Personality clashes can hinder the process, but are avoidable if you consider each person's individual style.

Working with people who communicate differently, or do anything differently, isn't a bad thing. Look at what's working for other people. Just because you didn't think of it first doesn't mean it isn't good. I've seen succession plans blow up when a person realized the company they are merging with doesn't do everything the same way they do. No advisor, team, or business will be exactly like you or yours. If you expect that, or expect them to change for you, you'll be sorely disappointed. If you are careful, however, you can find a good fit.

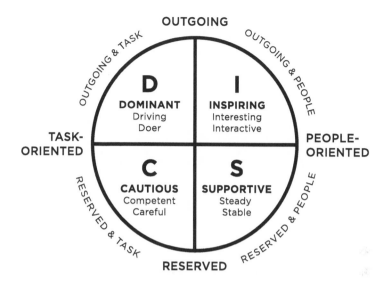

OUTGOING

OUTGOING & TASK

OUTGOING & PEOPLE

D
DOMINANT
Driving
Doer

I
INSPIRING
Interesting
Interactive

TASK-
ORIENTED

PEOPLE-
ORIENTED

C
CAUTIOUS
Competent
Careful

S
SUPPORTIVE
Steady
Stable

RESERVED & TASK

RESERVED & PEOPLE

RESERVED

Assessments like DiSC show you how people's different personalities can comple-ment each other for synergy, teamwork, and more productive working relationships.

Relationships

Look at the success of the relationships within the busi-ness's own staff and between them and their clients. Evaluate their personalities, processes, structures, the team, the value, and the price. Think about how they line up with yours. Relationships are a key differentiator in this business, especially those you have with your clients. Some are "nervous Nellies" who constantly need to be talked off the ledge. Other clients don't worry about the money much at all—they just want to know they can trust the advisor with it. Some clients require ten touches a year, while others don't want to be bothered more than once annually. A government employee or military member's preferences are usually very different from a corporate executive's financial interests. One leans toward safety, security, annuities, pensions, and spousal benefits. The other looks for growth, is more risk tolerant, and is less sensitive to market volatility.

An older gentleman who was merging with a business I was consulting for didn't seem to get along with anyone. Jonathan and the CEO always butted heads. Transitioning out of your business can be stressful, and Jonathan's short temper added to the tension. They had similar communication styles, which sometimes made it difficult to connect. The two men managed to do the deal, but during the handoff, they had to find a way to work together. I advised them to team Jonathan up with Jennifer, an advisor who I believed would complement his communication style. Jonathan still called the CEO regularly, and they still rubbed one another the wrong way. One day he told the CEO, "I feel like no one on your team understands anything I say, except for Jennifer."

He told him, "Well, that's not a coincidence. The reason Jennifer understands you and is getting everything done is because, on the advice of our consultant, we chose her for you. After working with you, I knew you would have a very difficult time with the way I receive and deliver information, and I'd have a hard time with the way you receive and deliver information. I paired you with a really great listener who can bring your information to me, then we can make decisions as a team. She delivers that information to you in a way that you understand." We always recommend adding *personality* to this process, and this is a perfect example of why.

Personality is imperative when you're looking at combining your practice, creating a succession plan, and even being acquired. While you're in the process, look ahead five years and ask yourself, "In a perfect world, what will the business look like? If I see a client in the grocery store, will they see me as a hero? Will they see the advisor they're working with now as a hero?" This is what you want. In the end, you should be able to look them in the eye knowing you did everything within your power to leave them in a good position with their advisory team.

GET TO KNOW THE POTENTIAL BUYERS

When you're vetting offers from acquiring businesses, look closely at what each one has to offer. Companies that do an internal review may not provide you with the best option, and it may not even be as profitable. Companies might require you to distribute it amongst multiple advisors, or they might have a set price that they're going to give you, and that's it. Some companies will pay you out as an employee, and others will pay you out as an independent business owner. Every company wants to strike a deal, and you'll hear a lot of them say something like, "Hey, I'll buy your book. Let's do a five- or seven-year buyout, and you can slowly ease away." This presents no risk to the person buying the book, but the risk to you is that it takes forever. People like Jack and Tom, whose time-lines have shrunk, have to make a decision more quickly than they would like to. This can cause the advisor a lot of undue stress.

Another thing to look for is the diversity and the age of the people in the business. In a conversation with Jack, he told me, "All the other firms that I interviewed were filled with men roughly ten years younger than me, in their late-60s and 70s. I didn't feel like I was providing my clients and their families—their children and grand-children—with a long-term strategy." The prospect of having his clients transitioned to a new business this year, and then again in another few years, disturbed him. His clients and their families represented individuals across a diverse spectrum of ages, races, religions, and genders, and he wanted to make sure they were being serviced by people who understood their needs and would stick with them for the long haul.

Another red flag is a business that isn't willing to explain their processes to you. They might tell you they have a process that's worked well for years, but unless they can explain their contact management strategy for transitioning and maintaining your clients, their process is not going to work. They may just be winging it for all you know.

QUESTIONS TO ASK A BUYER

1. Can you actually afford to buy my business?

2. Tell me about how you plan to actually transition these clients.

3. How important are face-to-face appointments versus phone appointments?

4. Is it important to keep a presence and have an office open here or is it important for the back office to be run there?

5. What is most important to you about how you run your business and interact with clients?

6. Describe a day in the life of your business. What happens from 9 to 5?

7. Describe a typical appointment with a client.

Another issue that can waste a lot of your time is the number of companies that want to talk to you about buying your business, but they can't even afford it. If you don't have ready access to this information, don't be afraid to bring in an outside organization that specializes in working with both parties for an easier and more transparent transition. Beyond the finances, get to know the potential buyers as people, too, and see if you share the same mentality toward clients. You can't assume that every company has a client-first mentality. Many do not.

Ultimately, no business will be a perfect match with yours, so you have to consider what's most important and prioritize. Beyond that, build a relationship with the buyer and work out the details. Whomever you choose to go with, you'll be dealing with them for a while, so make it a good relationship. Whether you're selling your business or merging with another one, keep it friendly and don't make assumptions when something isn't clear. Ask questions.

Your relationship isn't going to give you everything you want, exactly how you want it, but it can be a pleasant, productive, and profitable relationship for everyone. When I acquire a business, I follow the process my team and I have developed because I know it works. We have a transition for advisors who aren't currently in our broker-dealers. We have a process for how they acclimate with us. We have a plan. We make sure our clients are a match. We make sure our personalities are a match. We compare personality assessments to identify who on our team is the best person to work with the seller. Again, the ideal outcome is for the seller to be a hero to their clients, so everything we do is with that goal in mind. Done right, they're happy and their clients feel appreciated. We are going to be working with their clients, remember, and so this is also to our benefit. We want them to know that we care enough about them to make the transition as smooth and painless as possible, and they are confident that we will continue to care about them, as our clients.

CHAPTER EIGHT QUESTIONS

1. Your exit strategy may be selling your business (acquisition), creating a continuity plan (succession), or aligning and merging with another company (affiliation). To help you decide which of these is your best option, think about your current situation and the situations of your staff. Then consider the following questions:

     a. If you leave the business, will your staff stay on?
     b. If you leave, will your clients remain?
     c. If something happened to you, would the business continue or would it be decimated?

2. If you elect to merge your business with another firm, what do they want the outcome to look like?

3. What's a good timeline? What's your financial objective?

4. Are you compatible with this other firm?

CHAPTER 9

Letting Go

*Seek not that the things which happen should happen
as you wish; but wish the things which happen to be as they
are, and you will have a tranquil flow of life.*
—Epictetus

Nancy was a financial advisor with one of the big firms
that we all know. She'd been with their Chicago office
for decades. Approaching her sixtieth birthday, she wasn't
ready to end her career, but she wanted to scale back and
free up time for other activities. Working less would meet
her objectives, but how to do it?

She thought about what she liked and didn't like about
her situation. She loved her work and didn't want to abandon her clients. But she'd been spending time in Arizona
recently. The market there appealed to her, along with the
warm, dry weather.

She found a company that was positioned to help her
achieve her goals and her dreams. They weren't just focused on their own outcome with buying the business—
they talked to Nancy about what she wanted her outcome

to be as well. So she took some time to explore what her next stage could look like.

THE NEXT CHAPTER

Nancy was a wife, a mom, and a grandmother, and she wanted more time for the people she cared about most. She thought about what it would be like to relocate to the West where they could all enjoy a healthier outdoor lifestyle. Nancy genuinely didn't want to be completely disconnected from her clients, but she needed to disconnect enough to allow the new company to merge her business into their own: the people, the processes, and the systems. A smooth transition would make her the hero of her succession story. What if she could move to Arizona, but still stick around Chicago a few months a year to meet with clients, while the majority of her day-to-day tasks were managed by the back office and by other advisors.

Ultimately, Nancy structured a deal to stay on as an advisor, negotiating a deal with a ten-year payout where she draws a six-figure annual salary that allowed her to semi-retire in comfort. The company she merged with takes care of a lot of the work, but she still sees her Chicago clients in the summer and enjoys the rest of her time in Arizona, where she has a home now and spends most of the year. She put a pool in the backyard where she and her husband entertain friends, and they both play a lot more golf than they did back in Illinois. Her daughter and son-in-law are thinking of moving there next year so Nancy and her husband can spend more time with the grandkids.

Nancy didn't just quit being an advisor or hand over the keys to her business. She took control of her succession by envisioning her ideal next stage and finding a company that would work with her to make it a reality.

The hardest part for an advisor involved in a merger like this is letting go, and you don't have to—not completely, and at least not all at once. But you do have to realize that you're not alone anymore and you have people to count on who are going to be just as dedicated to your clients as you have been. You have to *allow* them to do that by creating a level of connectivity between yourself and the new team. Do that, and you can create continuity for your clients so they're still getting the service they expect and deserve. Then you can stop worrying and, eventually, let go.

WHAT DOES FREEDOM MEAN TO YOU?

If you've read this far, you know that I love what I do as a financial advisor and leader and CEO of an advisory company. And that I spend a lot of my time doing it. When you love what you do, it doesn't feel like work. It's what you'd be doing even if you didn't have to. I often think people who tell me I work too much are spending their time doing work they don't love, and they assume everyone is in that same position. But we're not.

If you're like me, you've found real passion and joy in working and helping your clients. When it's time to move on to your next stage, you don't have to stop doing what you love. You just have to make a continuity plan so you know what's next for you and those people who depend on you. At some point, it's time to let go of the old way of working and find passion and joy in other parts of your life.

That might be spending more time with your family, playing golf, and entertaining friends, like Nancy is doing. You might have other interests like working in the garden or joining a community organization that helps people in a different way than you're used to. If you plan well, your strategy allows you to let go of the old way of working and step into this new life that's just as fulfilling, with no disruption to your clients.

The bottom line is, ask yourself what freedom means to you. That word means different things to different people. For some, freedom means financial freedom: the freedom to make choices in life without being limited by money. It's the ability to pick the best choice, instead of the least expensive choice. Freedom can mean the freedom to separate from work. Not everyone wants to stop working altogether right away; they just want a plan in place so they can move on when the time comes. Still, other people see freedom as continuing to work as hard and as much as they always have, but in a different role—teaching what they know to others, for example. Think of the golfers who become golf coaches and the NBA stars who become basketball coaches. That kind of freedom allows you to unlock your potential at a whole new level.

Letting go means sacrificing something, but you have to give something up to get something in return. Often, when you let go, you temporarily give up money for time.

TRADING MONEY FOR TIME

In your next stage, you probably won't make the kind of income you're used to making. But you will have time. This isn't a normal place for a financial advisor to be—giving up money for time. It feels strange. Many successful people feel the same way.

I'll never forget my client Roger. He was in his mid-sixties and working in a job that paid very well, but which he absolutely hated. Roger's frustration and anger with work spilled over into our discussions, and I wanted to help him figure out how to retire. I did a financial plan, and it was obvious that Roger could stop working immediately and be financially set. Yet, he didn't want to quit his job. I could not understand what was going on. He hated his work, could afford to retire, yet refused to.

Roger finally opened up to me: his two adult daughters were living at home, and he was helping support them and their kids. He worked so much that he seldom had any quality time with them, but as long as his children and grandchildren relied on him for financial support, he felt he couldn't afford to retire.

I told Roger, "Listen, you hate your job. You're too tired at the end of the day to have fun with your grandchildren. Yet, you're unwilling to exchange the amount of *money* you're providing to them for *time* you could be spending with them." A side effect of Roger's support was that his children weren't motivated to support themselves, so in a way, he was enabling them to stay dependent on him and preventing them from enjoying the sense of responsibility and pride that might come with having their own careers and providing for their kids. They had so much unrealized potential and no compelling reason to explore it.

After some time, Roger stepped away from his job to establish a life for himself outside of work and spend more time with his family. He didn't do it right away. When you've been earning a certain income, it's difficult to make the choice to stop, to allow yourself the freedom to choose something else, *even when it's something you want so much more*. In Roger's case, he wanted more from life, and his family needed more from him, just not more money. His daughters needed a chance to take more responsibility for their family's finances, and his grandchildren needed him in their lives.

Roger retired, and now he has the freedom he desired— the freedom to spend time with his family and watch his grandchildren grow up. He's teaching them how to play baseball, and he takes them to the museum. And when they're playing on their own, Roger is putting time into lost hobbies from his past. His daughters still live with him, but they're working part-time, and they know they can count on their dad to help out with the kids whenever they ask. When I talk with him these days, Roger is truly happy. His kids are happier, and his wife is happier too. She has more time with her husband to do all the things they've been working toward for decades.

Defining what freedom means to you is a powerful exercise. While you're thinking about your freedom and how your current job status limits it, consider your partner's freedom. Are they missing out on their definition of freedom because of your choices? They may envision spending more time with you, sharing a hobby, taking mini-vacations, or joining a club together, but your drive to stick to the schedule you've been on for decades is preventing them from that freedom.

We're all getting older. As we approach our next stage, the opportunity to spend time with those we love gets shorter. People get sick. They die. I know advisors who waited so long to let go, their spouses were too sick to enjoy quality time with them. You married this person whom you love more than anyone else in the world—don't they deserve more than a few years of your time? Letting go when the time is right for you and your family is much more valuable than a few price points on your practice. If you're still questioning the value of time versus money, think about how much you made in the last year. What would it be worth to you to give that up, and trade it for a year with your spouse, your children, your grandchildren? Was the money as valuable as the time you sacrificed?

I know this is a difficult decision. I've talked to advisors pulling down a million or more a year, and it's tough to step away from that kind of cash. Taking the time to think about what freedom means to you—really means to you—will make the decision easier, maybe obvious. This is your life, and you are in control and can leave on your own terms—but be willing to let go!

WHY LETTING GO IS HARD

Money isn't the only reason people struggle with letting go. There are the relationships, too, with your employees, business associates, and your clients. Yes, those are all valuable, but if you have a succession plan in place, those people will be just fine. It's the people at home who have devoted their lives to you that deserve your time now. You may think your only value to them is the money you bring in, but that's not why they stuck with you all these years.

AN EXERCISE IN PRIORITIES

If you think you can't afford to work less, or let go completely, track your expenses for the next two weeks. Use your favorite notes app on your smartphone, and every time you buy something, write it down. After the two weeks are up, look at your list and add up all the expenses that weren't really necessary. How much money did you spend, and if you hadn't spent that money, could you afford to stop working and actually have a life that reflects your definition of freedom? What you might find is that you have plenty of money to do all those things you want to do in life, but you have to prioritize, and that means resisting the urge to spend frivolously, and dedicating your cash intentionally.

The same is true for how you spend your time. Log your time for two weeks and see what you're doing with all those precious minutes. How much time did you dedicate to the good stuff and how much time was spent doing things you didn't enjoy or don't serve you? Are you doing what you want to do, or have you fallen into a routine? How closely does that routine match your definition of freedom?

You might feel like you love your job, but when you look at that list, how much of your job do you really love and how much isn't really fun at all? You've been helping people in your role as an advisor, and that part of your job probably feels really good, right? There's no reason you can't continue helping people in a different capacity.

If you want to get serious about this, pick the day you think you'll leave this earth. Be honest with yourself—how much longer do you have? How many years, months, days? What do you want to do with that time? Is there anything you currently spend time on right now that you should stop doing? And what about those things you never have time for? Do you think you might be able to find time for them between now and your last day of life?

If you don't know what lights you up, it's because you just haven't asked yourself the question. Because you really do know the answer, if you think about it. Take a moment to think about a time when you were really truly happy. Take five minutes, half an hour. What were you doing that made you feel good inside, and what would you like to do more of with your time on earth? Is there anything you've always wanted to accomplish but are just waiting for that "right time?" That time is now.

Letting go doesn't take away from everything you've done. You're still a person who had an amazing career and helped a lot of people reach their financial goals. When you're ready to let go, think about all that you've accomplished and be grateful for that opportunity. You can't move forward without gratitude for where you've been. Be thankful for the journey you've been on, and for the journey that still awaits you. Be grateful for the moment you're in now.

Gratitude will serve you at any stage in your life, but appreciation isn't necessarily an automatic response for most people. Being intentional about what you're grateful for can reset your way of thinking. Start each day by writing down three things that you're grateful for. You can use a notebook or something like the *SELF Journal* by BestSelf, a planner that helps you identify your priorities beyond the day-to-day tasks.

DISCIPLINE EQUALS FREEDOM

> *Through discipline comes freedom.*
> —Aristotle

We all believe we're so disciplined and productive every day, but I'll tell you when I'm the most disciplined: the week before I go on vacation and the week I get back from vacation. It is simply amazing the amount of work I accomplish in those two weeks.

Aristotle's concept about discipline and freedom seems counterintuitive to an advisor early in their career.

Discipline, and having to abide by a set of rules, seems in fact to be the polar opposite of freedom. Freedom, it seems, *should* mean being at liberty to make all your own decisions.

It does, actually. But without imposing a level of self-control on yourself and your schedule, you cannot achieve the freedom to do or get what you truly want. Starting a firm or a career, we're all very disciplined—just like that week before we head off on vacation. We're so focused, goal-oriented, and practically immune from distractions because we see the prize: learning the job, launching the business, going to Hawaii. That discipline subsides over time, and advisors are left with a very undisciplined way of working. How do we recalibrate and get the discipline back into our work that makes us so productive?

I've always been somewhat disciplined, but like any advisor, my focus has lapsed too. At a point in my career, I made the conscious decision to get extremely organized and impose a strong sense of discipline on myself. I scheduled my appointments during certain months and set a weekly schedule with client meetings during certain times of certain days. I set aside days for community work, so I could tackle all the big rocks for the wine festival and other events. I didn't feel burdened by this schedule at all—it was empowering.

Having the day laid out for me allowed me to take control and gave me the freedom I thought I could achieve by not having a schedule. Instead of relying on total freedom in my schedule, I needed that schedule and the discipline to follow it to be productive. It gave me the freedom I desired.

As I became more disciplined in my approach and my practice—creating schedules, systems, and processes—I could take time off. My kids were out of school in July, so as I mentioned earlier, I decided to work half-days, not schedule any reviews, and take a family vacation that month every year. This was the one time in the year when I could disconnect from work and really focus on myself and my family. That discipline also created a more predictable experience for my clients and for my team.

We created a client relationship management workflow—the Freedom Street Contact Management System mentioned earlier—for maximizing touches to clients; by utilizing this system to automate and manage the process we were able to elevate our services. My systematic approach to doing business liberated me from worrying about what wasn't getting done, or who wasn't being called. It freed my mind and my time because once I'd accomplished everything I'd set out to do, I could relax and do whatever I wanted, confident that nothing had been missed or forgotten.

A DISCIPLINED APPROACH TO YOUR BUSINESS

You create individual plans for your clients, but having some structure in how you create those plans makes the process easier, repeatable, and prevents the odds of missing important considerations in those plans. I've mentioned having a call cycle, where you schedule contacts with clients at specific times of the year to talk through matters such as life in general and specific topics such as income, risk, and performance. Depending on the client base, it may take your team a month to work through all those calls and then you can spend the next month following up on opportunities and life transitions uncovered during the calls. This method frees up the other weeks and months for everything else, including meeting with clients face-to-face, doing events, and working on your business. You might even take a vacation.

When I meet with a new advisor or firm that wants to merge with our business, one of my objectives is to identify what the advisor is doing really well. Then I look for what they're doing that I can improve by applying our company's systems. I show them how to implement our systems and processes, not to help them become the god of their business, but the prophet. I share what I know that can help them improve their business and align with mine. I empower them to improve, because I don't want them to rely on me and my team to do everything for them.

I also identify functions that can be more centrally managed, such as investment management, human resources, marketing, branding, compliance, and reviews. These are time-intensive activities that don't directly benefit the advisor, and where centralizing and streamlining can take a lot off their plate, freeing them up to do more that benefits their clients and their business.

DON'T MICROMANAGE EVERYTHING—
BELIEVE IN THE PROCESS AND MOVE ON

Discipline also gives you the freedom to plan your exit strategy. You need to know what you're doing from one day to the next before you can look ahead to your next stage with any kind of clarity. Planning your day, your week, your month—the next five years—and having the discipline to follow a plan frees you from worry and uncertainty. This approach also frees up time to explore new options outside of your schedule.

When I'm meeting with an advisor who's planning their next stage, we have to define what the next phase looks like. We have to establish a timeline. Most of all, we have to define what their role looks like in that next phase. This is where having a plan, systems, processes, and the discipline to follow this approach really pays off, because as long as you're involved in every day-to-day decision, constantly changing how and when things are done, you can never hand anything off and step away from the business.

A company that's defined, documented, tested, and has the discipline to follow systems, processes, and schedules empowers its employees. The company takes on a transparency so everyone understands "how things work." Contrast this approach with allowing tribal knowledge to develop within silos, which puts you at a risk if the only people with that knowledge take time off or leave the company. Secrecy around a company's systems within that company don't help anyone and, in fact, can promote a feeling of distrust. By providing transparency to your people and the acquiring company, you can exit the business with dignity, confident that you're leaving those people, your employees, and your clients in good hands and without fear of a disruption in service.

This also makes your business that much more attractive to the acquiring company and allows them to decide whether or not you'll be a good fit before you make the deal. Think of this process as premarital counseling: you tell them how you do things, and they decide whether your company and theirs are compatible.

Don't skip this step. Sometimes, advisors skip it for the same reason two people in love scoff at counseling. They'll work out the problems as they come to them. Love will solve everything. Except the selling advisors often believe that price will solve everything. That's not the case, and no matter how much a company is willing to pay for your business, you will deeply regret the deal if you're not upfront with them about how your business and theirs will ultimately merge.

Money is the bare minimum that you need to agree on before an acquisition or merger, just like being in love is the bare minimum for a couple to get married. Get to know the people who will be serving your customers and how they do business—the personalities and processes. If Mrs. Andrews is used to a monthly call from you, who is going to be making that call and how are they going to treat Mrs. Andrews? That kind of thing. I worked with a firm that did all their meetings via videoconferencing, which is efficient for the advisors and clients, but if they were to take on another firm where clients expected face-to-face, in-person meetings, that would need to be discussed. How would the clients react, and does it make sense to take on a business with different practices?

It's easy to take the relationships you've developed with people for granted, but they are very real and, in many cases, they're what's kept you in business. I had a difficult client once who didn't click with me or some of my staff. I thought about why we rubbed one another the wrong way and decided to match him up with an advisor who I believed would best suit his personality. One day, the client called me and said, "Scott, I really want to thank you. Greg really seems to understand me." I just smiled and thanked him for the feedback, knowing that Greg—our most junior advisor—had been hand-picked by me to complement this client's personality quirks. If you are doing that for your clients and advisors, discuss it with the new firm. Talk to them about the relationships you've established with clients and why. Don't leave them or your clients blindsided, awkwardly trying to work together without the premarital counseling or even the love.

Another reason to talk through all these matters is because you have to start seeing the next stage. Beyond the paperwork and the money, you have to actually envision your clients working with other people and you moving on. I've seen advisors get "cold feet" as their date of separation approaches. Sometimes they want to back out. The next stage looks different and scary, and they have so much uncertainty. Have the meetings, have the talks. Discuss who does the laundry, who takes the dog for a walk, and whose turn it is to take out the trash, then move on to your next stage, confident that your business, your team, and your clients are going to be happy with the new arrangement. The ideal result is a business that continues without you in it, and people see you as the hero who made that outcome possible.

LEVELING UP

Moving on and letting go is easier when you level up. This can mean leaving toxic people and places behind that may have worked for you in the past, but don't serve you well now and have no place in your future. Leveling up is important because unless you give up what you don't want or need, you won't have space for everything you want and need in your next stage. Once you level up, you won't want to level back down.

Leveling up is how lottery winners and professional athletes survive the abrupt changes in their financial statuses. They may have people in their lives who believe that since their friend won the lottery or earned the right to play professional sports, they did too—and deserve a stake in all the benefits that come with it. This can happen to you too, and you may have to step away from some people to make room for new people who are on your level, in similar situations and with aspirations like yours.

People are on different journeys in their lives, and when you let go, it could serve you well to let go of people who are on a much different journey than yours. If you don't, it's going to be very hard to move on.

Think about how it was when you went to college or landed your first job at a good firm. You earned the right to go to college or work at that company, and you have to look out for yourself and make sure you fulfill the expectations of that school or business. That may not be possible if you're still hanging with the old crew at the same old places. I'm not suggesting you desert your friends, but if you're at a point in life where the people you surround yourself with no longer share your values or your goals, it might be time to level up to new friends who do.

Leveling up means giving up old habits too. We all get into ruts like having dinner every month with that couple we don't have anything in common with, or going to that annual spaghetti dinner because our colleagues expect us to go. It means quitting positions that aren't in line with our definition of freedom. Are you on a board that represents something you couldn't care less about? Maybe it's time to quit that board. Maybe there's another board that supports a cause you're crazy about but have never had time for. Well, there you go. Quit that board you hate and join the one you love. Or quit the board and do something entirely different with your time. It's up to you.

LETTING GO GRADUALLY

A successful strategy for letting go is to do it gradually. Work three days a week and take Friday through Monday off, or work half-days several times a week.

Take an extended vacation. You probably haven't done that in a while. That two-week trip to Europe or New Zealand that you've always wanted to go on but never seemed to have the time. If your business is in order for your next stage, go on that trip. See how it feels, and how it works out for your office team and your clients. It's sort of like sending your kids to camp for two weeks and seeing how they make out. If you've taught them how to behave and take care of themselves, they'll do fine. But if you've allowed them to rely on you for every decision, they may have some problems. When you're ready to step away, you should have prepared your team for that—for the good, for the bad, and for the surprises.

Don't forget to make new friends, too. When you're in business with a group of people for years, they become your best friends, and while you don't need to abandon those friendships, you should look ahead to whom you can add to your life. Whatever you're going to do in the next stage, seek out others who share your interests. You don't want to be the guy or gal who still shows up at the office every week to hang out because you're lonely and don't have any other friends.

Letting go isn't just ending one chapter—it's starting a new one. Rather than looking back on what you're giving up, look ahead to what you have to gain, because suddenly you have time for it.

CHAPTER NINE QUESTIONS

1. What does freedom mean to you?

2. Do you love to travel? Do you wish you could spend more time with your spouse and other family? Do you have friends outside of work whom you'd like to hang out with more? What about hobbies that you've abandoned, people you'd like to help, or charities or causes you'd like to support, but never had the time?

3. What would having the freedom to do all these things be like? What does having the freedom to live your life, your way, really mean?

PART III ACTION PLAN

1. Have a notebook for writing all your thoughts about what's next for you. Take some "thinking time" each day to consider your career and how you will get to Freedom Street. Put your phone away and use an old-school egg timer instead to set enough time for this activity and write as much as you can. You might begin your notebook by deciding which stage you are in within your career: rookie, midpoint, or seasoned advisor. Then, think about why you got into this business. Have your original goals been met? Also think about your current situation as an advisor: does it make sense for you to be an employee or should you strike out on your own? Do you like the people you work with, and are you serving the clients you want to serve? Or is it time for a change? You can also use your thinking time and notebook to accomplish activities that require a certain level of concentration. Here are some examples:

   a. Identify a certain client and the strategies behind what you're trying to accomplish.
   b. Visualize where you see the month or the quarter going.
   c. Think about issues you have with your staff and how you can solve them.

2. Make a plan to level up. Identify people with whom you'd like to surround yourself, those people who share your interests and values you believe in and are at the level you're aiming to achieve. Find out where these people are and how you can network

with them. Delete the toxic people and make time for those people that add more value to your life.

3. Begin to let go of your current schedule if it's crazy and undisciplined. Create repeatable processes and a schedule that allows you to work just four days a week instead of five and explore your definition of freedom on that other day.

Conclusion

*Be who God meant you to be
and you will set the world on fire.*
—Saint Catherine of Siena

I talk with a lot of advisors. What I hear from them is what drove me to write this book. It's not so much the numbers that they worry about, or the money, or even the financial security. What advisors—and business owners in general—struggle with is their next stage of life. They want to know what tomorrow looks like. They want to know what all their options are, and what to do today to make their best option a reality.

People want to look back on their accomplishments without regret, while creating opportunities for life beyond work. I call the process Life and Wealth Optimization. You would think doing this is natural for advisors, because it's essentially what we do for our clients every day. But putting yourself on the other side of the table, asking yourself all those questions, putting together a plan, and then executing on it is not always as simple as it seems. Think about how your own clients struggle with it, and how you guide and support them through it all.

Think about how long you've been doing this for other people. You've had clients in their 20s, 30s, 40s, and older rely on you to step them from their early careers to end of life. You helped them make sure their kids could go to college. You showed them how to budget their time and money so they could afford those vacations. And when there were downturns in the market and their investments lost value—or the client lost their job—you were there to remind them that this was temporary. Thanks to the plan you put together for them and their diligence adhering to it, they will weather the storm.

You were part of their finances, their career, and their life. Maybe you have one of their kids working for you now, and you helped them set up the grandkids' 529s. You've been involved in the lifecycles of all these people, and you didn't just juggle the numbers for them—you gave them the plan and the confidence to charge ahead into their next phase.

You told them when they could or couldn't retire, and *how* they could do it. You told them when they could take more money in retirement because they weren't taking enough. You gave them the confidence to take more when they weren't taking any. Sometimes, you advised people that they were taking too much and needed to pull back. Whatever guidance you provided, you did it with confidence because you knew what you were talking about.

You've made a difference in the lives of hundreds, maybe thousands of families across the country, and with future generations around the world. People are more financially stable—financially free—because of you and your informed, confident advice. I want you to have that same confidence charging ahead in the next chapter of your own life. You can create a strategy for making your next stage the best one possible and do so with the same level of confidence that you provided all those people throughout your career.

Now it's time for you to take your own advice. Now is the time to execute on what you believe in. Now, what you've learned and talked about your entire career, you have to actually *do*. For yourself. Learning, knowing, teaching, guiding, and supporting are different than *acting*. To prepare for the next stage, for your own financial freedom—whether it's by succession, a merger, or even selling outright your practice and being acquired—you will have to evaluate the execution and the action steps required. Just like you've taught your clients to evaluate all the plans you put in place for them and the actions they had to take to make them work.

That's what I'm asking you to do with this book: ask yourself what freedom means to you. So few of us live our lives with real freedom because we don't define it or take steps to live it. But we can all make freedom our next stage.

You might be an advisor who spent your entire career doing all the things you dreamed of. You've been on vacations. You've seen your kids grow up. You never missed anything. You defined what matters to you, and you lived it. Now, it's time to decide how you will spend more time living that way, and with a plan for your business that allows you to move into that next stage with peace of mind.

The alternative is what too many people settle for: thinking they'll figure it all out later, or that they'll do nothing and everything will magically work out. You're not going to work forever, especially the way you're working right now. No one does. The time to start creating your rich life, living your legacy, and owning your future is now.

Plan for what you want and start to execute on the very advice you would give your clients. Flip the table and sit on the other side: What is the best advice you would give yourself right now?

To create a rich life, you have to define a rich life. Define it, create it, enjoy it. Start living your legacy today and making an impact on whatever is important to you. What matters most can no longer be put off for later. Execute today, so that as you transition to the next chapter, you'll have that fulfilling life and a road map for how you'll spend your time going forward.

It takes discipline to get all of this in place, but as an advisor, you have some mastery of discipline already and the potential to be even more disciplined. Once you move into that next stage, buy into it fully. Embrace it, and let the rest go.

If you still have doubts, think about this: you've made a career out of getting people to trust you so you can help them. Isn't it time you trusted yourself to do the same for you? If you don't have the best plan yet, that's okay—start today. Do it yourself or hire a consultant or coach who can help you with it—hold you accountable, question it, and shoot holes into it until you get it right.

Don't be afraid to ask for help. This is your life we're talking about.

I wouldn't be doing my job if I didn't tell you that I do this for a living. My team and I guide advisors through their next chapter, and it's some of the most rewarding work I do. Check us out at scottdanner.com.

And if you're still feeling uncomfortable, check out the case studies in the appendix. These are examples of advisors in different scenarios with whom we've worked to help them move to their next stage. You might see yourself in some of these stories, or you might have your own story to tell. Let's make it a story with a happy ending. You've got this.

Recommended Reading and Resources

As an avid reader, I'm inspired by the wisdom and guidance of authors who have documented their own experiences and learnings for the benefit of others. I'm also open to advice from my colleagues, mentors, and the many people in my networking circle—especially those with goals similar to my own.

Here are just a few of the many books, people, and businesses whose guidance I've found very valuable on my Freedom Street journey.

Cunningham, Keith J. *The Road Less Stupid: Advice from the Chairman of the Board*. Austin: Keys to the Vault, 2017.

Dalio, Ray. *Principles: Life and Work*. New York: Simon & Schuster, 2017.

Duckworth, Angela. *Grit: The Power of Passion and Perseverance*. New York: Simon & Schuster, 2016.

Duhigg, Charles. *The Power of Habit: Why We Do What We Do in Life and Business.* New York: Random House, 2012.

Frankl, Viktor E. *Man's Search for Meaning.* Boston: Beacon, 2006.

Grau, David, Sr. *Buying, Selling, and Valuing Financial Practices: The FP Transitions M&A Guide + Website.* Hoboken: Wiley, 2016.

Grau, David, Sr. *Succession Planning for Financial Advisors: Building an Enduring Business + Website.* Hoboken: Wiley, 2014.

Herold, Cameron. *Meetings Suck: Turning One of the Most Loathed Elements of Business into One of the Most Valuable.* Austin: Lioncrest, 2016.

Herold, Cameron. *Vivid Vision: A Remarkable Tool for Aligning Your Business Around a Shared Vision of the Future.* Austin: Lioncrest, 2017.

Hill, Napoleon. *Think and Grow Rich Deluxe Edition: The Complete Classic Text.* New York: TarcherPerigee, 2008.

Knight, Phil. *Shoe Dog: A Memoir by the Creator of Nike.* New York: Scribner, 2016.

Long, Randy M. *The BraveHeart Exit: 7 Steps to Your Family Business Legacy.* Las Vegas: Next Century, 2016.

Maxwell, John C. *The 15 Invaluable Laws of Growth: Live Them and Reach Your Potential*. New York: Hachette, 2012.

Maxwell, John C. *The 21 Irrefutable Laws of Leadership: Follow Them and People Will Follow You*. Nashville: Thomas Nelson, 2007.

Moeller, Steve. *Effort-Less Marketing for Financial Advisors: Five Steps to a Super-Profitable Business and a Wonderful Life*. Tustin: American Business Visions, 1999.

Oechsli, Matt. *Becoming a Rainmaker: Creating a Downpour of Serious Money*. Overland Park: Wealth Management, 2006.

Oechsli, Matt, and Stephen Boswell. *Best Practices of Elite Advisors: The Relationship Management/Relationship Marketing Nexus*. Overland Park: Wealth Management, 2013.

Palaveev, Philip. *The Ensemble Practice: A Team-Based Approach to Building a Superior Wealth Management Firm*. Hoboken: Wiley, 2013.

Soforic, John. *The Wealthy Gardener: Lessons on Prosperity Between Father and Son*. New York: Portfolio, 2020.

Voss, Chris and Tahl Raz. *Never Split the Difference: Negotiating As If Your Life Depended On It*. New York: HarperCollins, 2016.

Disclosure

The information contained in this book does not purport to be a complete description of the securities, markets, or developments referred to in this material. The information has been obtained from sources considered to be reliable, but we do not guarantee that the foregoing material is accurate or complete. Any information is not a complete summary or statement of all available data necessary for making an investment decision and does not constitute a recommendation. Any opinions of the chapter author are those of the chapter author and not necessarily those of Freedom Street Partners. Expressions of opinion are as of the initial book publishing date and are subject to change without notice.

Freedom Street Partners is not responsible for the consequences of any particular transaction or investment decision based on the content of this book. All financial, retirement, and estate planning should be individualized as each person's situation is unique.

This information is not intended as a solicitation or an offer to buy or sell any security referred to herein. Keep in mind that there is no assurance that our recommendations or strategies will ultimately be successful or profitable nor protect against a loss. There may also be the potential for missed growth opportunities that may occur after the sale of an investment. Recommendations, specific investments, or strategies discussed may not be suitable for all investors. Past performance may not be indicative of future results. You should discuss any tax or legal matters with the appropriate professional.

Acknowledgments

When I think of all the people who have helped me—either directly or indirectly—write this book, I cannot even begin to list everyone's name. If you and I had an interaction, a meeting, or even a moment, I have remembered it and it has mattered to me and to this story.

In the same way that I prioritize my time and my love in four quadrants, I'd like to acknowledge some of these people by all they've contributed, and the difference they've made, to my Life, my Work and Wealth, my Health, and my Spirit.

I want to start with *Life*! I cannot thank my family enough. That includes my mother and father for laying the groundwork of my life so lovingly, and to my siblings, cousins, aunts, and uncles. I lived with some of them over the years, pulled energy from others, and was picked up by plenty of them. I am a living example of a village-raised man. I am so grateful for all of the early days and our close-knit family. I never would have even known what an entrepreneur was without my uncles teaching me about business and showing me the courage to take it on. As for my aunts, they are mentioned a ton in this book, but they can never be mentioned enough. Derek and Stephanie, I love our story.

Adrienne and my boys are mentioned early; you all are my purpose and my present. I am who I am because of the other half of my marriage. I am held together with a balanced partner and two kids, and I couldn't be happier to have you in my life, or more proud.

Next, I have to mention the people who have made my *Work* so fulfilling. My partners at Freedom Street, Andrew and Reed: a huge thanks to you two for believing in me so much. None of this, meaning the story or the book, is complete without the team. Valerie and our FSP team of advisors, back office, and friends. You all are so important to me, thank you. Renee, thanks for helping me limp across the finish line!

To LWO, all of you are part of this big playbook, and I am so thankful for our partnerships. Ryan and Matty, Trav and team, thanks! Raymond James, thanks for allowing me to bring my story to life.

Thanks, too, to my previous firm and all of my friends still there. You let me grow up and fail often in leadership, as well as grow into the leader I am today. Thanks for the guidance and friendships that are the foundation I now stand on.

Health is so incredibly important to me, and I am just so grateful to be healthy enough to live life the way I do. I have the energy to take on the world, and I am thankful for the investment I've made in my health, and to everyone who's supported me along the way. Most of all, thank God!

Finally, I'd like to address the fourth quadrant, *Spirit*. Without God, I am nothing. In Him, I find all strength, and my ultimate goal is to use my talents in life to make a difference here on Earth so that one day I will see Him. I am very spiritual, and I am so thankful for the early Catholic school education and for my parents' guidance to stay focused on God and something bigger than myself. That has always grounded me, and I feel very blessed.

If you are reading this book, watching my videos, or investing any time in what I create, I pray that it helps you reach your goals and dreams. I'm grateful for you. Thanks for taking the time to get all the way to this part of the book!

About the Author

Scott Danner is first and foremost a family man who is very proud of his wife, Adrienne, their eighteen-year marriage, and their two boys. A spiritual man, Scott loves God and feels blessed to be in a career that allows him to share his gifts with others.

Scott is also the founder and leader of the Chesapeake Wine Festival, which attracts thousands of people annually and has generated millions of dollars for local charities. He also consults on major events for profit and for charitable causes including Boys and Girls Clubs, local schools and hospitals, and anywhere else he can lend a hand.

Scott's professional roles include CEO and founding partner of Freedom Street Partners, which he and the other founders have grown from zero to more than $2 billion AUM in less than five years. He is also a financial advisor and a top producer at Raymond James, where he is a chairman's council member and was named Forbes Best in State Virginia for 2020. Scott enjoys business consulting, and coaching and training financial advisors. He looks forward to leading Freedom Street Partners into the future by focusing on connection and relationships, and by following the company's core values of integrity, ownership, passion, and freedom. Their tagline, "Life Wealth Optimization," reminds Scott and his colleagues to put life first every day.

Scott says, "I'm always striving to be better, live better, and give more. I don't have it all figured out, but with every new connection, relationship, and conversation, I learn more every day. I'm very fortunate to be in a position to spread what I learn to help others be better, live better, and give more too."

Made in the USA
Las Vegas, NV
05 October 2021